G. I.
Jungle

AN AMERICAN SOLDIER
IN AUSTRALIA AND NEW GUINEA

by

E. J. KAHN, JR.

SIMON AND SCHUSTER
NEW YORK
1943

About the Appearance of Books in Wartime

A recent ruling by the War Production Board has curtailed the use of paper by book publishers in 1943.

In line with this ruling and in order to conserve materials and manpower, we are co-operating by:

1. Using lighter-weight paper, which reduces the bulk of our books substantially.
2. Printing books with smaller margins and with more words to each page. Result: fewer pages per book.

Slimmer and smaller books will save paper and plate metal and labor. We are sure that readers will understand the publishers' desire to co-operate as fully as possible with the objectives of the War Production Board and our government.

MANUFACTURED IN THE UNITED STATES OF AMERICA
BY THE VAIL-BALLOU PRESS, INC., BINGHAMTON, N. Y.

THIS BOOK IS DEDICATED

WITH AFFECTION AND RESPECT

TO

THE MEN OF THE 32D INFANTRY DIVISION

WHO TOOK BUNA

AND TO

MAJOR GENERAL E. F. HARDING

WHO LED THEM TO IT

ACKNOWLEDGMENTS

A good deal of the material in this book appeared originally in *The New Yorker*. For permission to reprint a few additional bits of prose that were once the exclusive property of military readers, the author is indebted to *Yank*, the Army Weekly.

PREFACE

THERE are now hundreds of thousands of American soldiers overseas, which is a good thing. This book is a somewhat dis-jointed account of the experiences of one of the men who were fortunate enough to get off to an early start. The division to which I belonged was among the first combat ele-ments of our Army to go to the Southwest Pacific and among the first to take the offensive anywhere. We left the United States, not long after Pearl Harbor, before anybody got around to handing us any of those instructive pamphlets now distributed to soldiers heading overseas to spare them the embarrassment of peeking under the veils of Moslem women or saying "bloody" to duchesses. Without benefit of the printed word of warning, we went to Australia and stayed there until we were sent to New Guinea. My outfit wounded practically no Australians and a great many Japanese, so I guess we did all right in both places, even without the pamphlets.

This is not a sight-seeing book. My pals and I saw as many sights as circumstances permitted, but our field of vision was limited. I cannot say exactly where we were stationed in Australia, but I can say that, to my regret, I never got to visit

Sydney. This omission on my part aroused some scathing comment from a world-traveled friend of mine who, on my return to New York, upbraided me severely, pointing out that anyone who got as close to Sydney as I did and failed to cover that last short lap ought to be ashamed of himself. Sydney would have been a nice sight to see, but I didn't get there, simply because I was never ordered there. Similarly, I have probably been guilty of slighting such scenic attractions as the moon shining on the Pacific off the north coast of Papua. It was doubtless a handsome moon, but whenever it was out we were worrying too much about enemy planes to pay rapt attention to its brilliance. We were probably not even so impressed by the New Guinea jungle itself as we should have been. The jungle, like so many other settings in which we found ourselves at one time or another, had its bizarre points, to be sure, but it was, after all, merely another billeting area to which we had temporarily been assigned by the Army in the course of performing our well-assorted duties. Its outlandishness was tempered by the fact that it was something the government had issued to us. It was a jungle which, in many small and intimate ways, soon assumed some of the characteristics of any plot of ground on which the Army pitches its tents. It was, in other words—in our own words— a G. I. jungle.

This book does not discuss the strategy and tactics of the war in general or even of the particular part of it in which I happened to be involved. It is not the business of the individual soldier to concern himself with the larger issues. The fact that a reader might get the lopsided impression from these pages that the Japanese were our only enemy is all right with me; over there, so far away from other theaters of war, the Japs *were* our only enemy. Of course, we were interested in the news from Russia and Africa, but in a detached way, as we might have been in the marriage of a girl we had gone out with once but hadn't heard from for ages.

This collection of pieces was written at various times and places. Some of the earlier chapters were composed on the stage of a barnlike theater in a South Australian army camp. The theater, built originally for the entertainment of Australian troops, who went to the Middle East before they had a chance to enjoy it, had never been used for anything until my outfit moved in and converted it into an office. I spent many a wintry night huddled in a draughty corner of the stage, and if there are any words that look as if they slipped into the opening passages from some other book, my excuse is that it was difficult to type with gloves on. Some of the book was written in another Australian camp, deep in woods once occupied mainly by wallabies, koalas, goannas, scorpions, and huge eucalyptus trees; some of it, in a dingy hotel room in Port Moresby; some of it, in the muddy jungle on the north side of the Owen Stanley Mountains, where I had to abandon one paragraph in the middle of a beautiful, irretrievable thought when a five-inch tarantula crawled up around the side of the portable and perched menacingly on the space bar. None of the book was written under front-line fire. My military duties compelled me to remain, during nearly all the time I was in New Guinea, some distance behind the really active areas. I never fired my rifle at a Japanese, and no

Japanese, to the best of my knowledge, ever fired his rifle at me. So, this is not the tale of a soldier in battle, except insofar as it is the tale of a soldier whose outfit was in battle and who got as close to things as his job let him.

Some people think that an author is solely responsible for his published handiwork. It ain't necessarily so. In this particular case, for instance, it would be base ingratitude for me not to single out—among the many people to whom I am thankful for having lent me a hand or a piece of paper to write on—William Shawn, of *The New Yorker*, without whose generous assistance and discriminating editorial eye it is a wonder to me that any writer can get along.

—E. J. K.

CONTENTS

1

Troopship

To CROSS an ocean in a convoy and find that the experience isn't as harrowing as you've been led to expect is something of an emotional letdown. I arrived in Australia early in May, 1942, after traveling on a troopship nonstop from San Francisco. During the extremely long voyage I never once had the sensation that I was in any immediate or acute danger, and neither, I think, did most of the several thousand other soldiers on the ship. We were all aware, of course, of the peculiarity of our situation. We knew that any enemy bomber pilot or submarine commander would have hissed with delight at the very sight of us. Every exterior inch of our ship was painted a drab, unassuming gray. For more than half of each day we were under total blackout conditions. The upper decks bristled with armament, and from time to time we would hear the comforting crackle of the antiaircraft gunners trying out their weapons. Our ship never stopped moving; anyone who has ever engaged in firing practice knows the advantages of a stationary target. We had been solemnly advised at the start of the voyage that should anyone have the misfortune to fall overboard, he would have to shift for

himself; the ship would not stop for him. We had been issued
lifebelts as soon as we got on board and began wearing them
five minutes before we sailed from our pier in California.
From that moment until shortly before we were safely tied up
at an Australian pier, our lifebelts were always within arm's
reach. Our cartridge belts, with canteens attached and filled
to the top, were always with us, too. In case we ever found
ourselves floating on an unprovisioned raft, we would at least
have a quart of fresh water apiece.

At frequent intervals we marched briskly on deck for
"abandon-ship" drills and stood in quiet, orderly rows while
the crew lowered and raised lifeboats. We spent one morning
climbing down knotted ropes that had been strung from an
upper deck to a lower one. We had orders that in the event
of an emergency we should leave the ship by means of such
ropes; we were urged not to jump into the water. It was
pointed out to us that if we did, our lifebelts would undoubtedly hit us in the chin and knock us cold. We took an interest
in these precautionary measures, but somehow we rarely
stopped to think about whether we would ever be called
upon to use them in order to save our lives. Our attitude was
not callous, indifferent, or frivolous; it was simply fatalistic.
We didn't joke much about the possibility of our being sunk;
we hardly mentioned it at all, though it was not considered
a particularly delicate issue. When, in a daily mimeographed
paper published aboard ship for the troops, the possibility
that the ship might be sunk happened to be brought up, the
readers were not shocked or offended. In fact, they joined an
enthusiastic discussion which went on in print for the next

few days, not about the ship's potential distress, which was held to be not worth wasting words on, but about whether a ship, if it did sink, would plummet straight to the bottom of the ocean or would stop somewhere on the way down. The controversy was settled in favor of the first premise by a learned officer, who submitted a treatise on the relative specific gravities of water and steel.

In addition to the paper, which kept us posted on such topical matters as how far the ship could sink, we received daily bulletins from the wireless operator, who dispensed résumés of war news, baseball scores, and other items radioed by the United Press, without whose thoughtfulness we might never have known, for instance, that a certain horsy couple back in the States had been married while astride their favorite mounts or that Margie Hart had left Hollywood in a huff. Our ship was not allowed to send any messages, since their transmission might have revealed our position, so we had to accept whatever news came through to us and could not ask any questions about doubtful points. The troops were not permitted to talk to the wireless operator, and thus they sampled only so much of his knowledge as was officially released, in addition to a small amount of auxiliary matter surreptitiously passed from deck to deck through the ever-flowing rumor channels. Undoubtedly the most diverting rumor was one indicating that a Japanese news commentator had been heard to claim the sinking of our transport, presumably as incidental to the Coral Sea battle, which was then in progress. This report was greeted with the usual laughter meted out by the informed to the tales of the ignorant until someone soberly pointed out what effect such a story, if published in the United States, could have upon our families, who, not having heard from us for some time, might logically suspect that we were at sea. One soldier, who used to work on a newspaper and had frequently insisted that even in wartime a minimum of curbs should be placed on the press, said he hoped the Army or Navy or somebody else would prevent his alma mater from publishing any such enemy claims, even when labeled as fantastic stories and without foundation. "That sort of thing ought to be censored," the soldier said firmly. Even a newspaperman feels differently about the news when he's it.

Perhaps the most reassuring feature of a convoy is the fact that there are other ships in it. An ocean is a large and lonely area. In peacetime people crossing on ships are given to rushing excitedly to the decks to gaze at a passing vessel, even a small and dowdy one. They wave happily at its passengers, regarding them all as fine, friendly folk. Traveling in a convoy, you always have company, so the water doesn't seem as boundless and frightening as it otherwise might. Wherever you step out on deck, you know that you'll see a friendly ship steaming along at your side, up ahead, or a stretch behind, occasionally tooting fraternally or blinking some intimate message.

The troopship I was on, like most of the others in our clubby group, had once been a handsome luxury liner operating in the Pacific, and its crew loved to reminisce about the old days, dwelling proudly on the celebrities, including Shirley Temple, who had graced its spacious cabins and lofty lounges. On

December 7, 1941, the ship was making a routine shuttle between Hawaii and California when the radio operator heard a faint and incredible SOS from a freighter three hundred miles away, which claimed to have been hit by a Japanese torpedo. An hour later the news of Pearl Harbor came through. The captain proceeded as rapidly as possible to San Francisco, where his passengers gratefully scurried ashore. The vessel hasn't carried a carefree celebrity since.

Before going into transport service, the ship was ruthlessly stripped of nearly all the trimmings that had made her comely and expensive. Only a few particularly fine bits of paneled wood were left in place and carefully boarded over. The outdoor swimming pool was drained and an antiaircraft gun was mounted in it. Gun crews on their way to their stations have since tramped across the fading outlines of a shuffleboard court. Every portable piece of furniture was removed to make room for berths; not even a piano was left on board. Staterooms once occupied by two vacationing passengers were converted into accommodations for nine, twelve, or even fifteen men. On the trip I made, soldiers slept on decks, in the lounge, in the grand ballroom, in the bar, and in every other habitable space. Most of us had canvas hammocks, slung in tiers of three or four from wooden or metal posts. I slept, for instance, on the top story of a three-decker job so close to the ceiling that if I absent-mindedly sat up in bed I bumped my head. On boarding the ship, I was assigned to a fifteen-man stateroom (my roommates and I shared a bathroom with a dozen fellows in an adjoining cabin), and when I was later shifted into a room containing only eight other soldiers, with a bath for our exclusive use, I felt that my new quarters were extravagantly commodious.

There is little privacy in an army at any time; on our ship privacy wasn't even a possibility. You couldn't go anywhere without running into a lot of people. Movement of any sort was circumscribed. Since a part of each end of the main promenade deck had been shut off to provide extra berth space, we were denied the time-honored nautical privilege of estimating the number of laps around the deck to a mile and seeing how many miles we could click off between breakfast and lunch. Even if the ends of the deck had been left open, walking around it would have been difficult, since no area was sufficiently free of lounging soldiers to be navigable. The men stood at the rail or sprawled on the deck flooring; there were no deck chairs on board this trip. Few of the soldiers had ever been on an ocean before, so many of them leaned on the rail for hours, trying to remember not to throw anything overboard—this was strictly forbidden lest the refuse form a trail by which our course might be discovered —and gazing with surprise and admiration at the changing aspects of the sea. Having no experience in ocean travel, they didn't miss the luxuries they did not know about. The crew, however, did miss them and would utter mournful laments now and then while trying to keep up with their accelerated duties. "Used to be fresh water in every bathroom faucet," a barber told me reflectively while cutting my hair, adding in awed tones that since the start of our voyage he had used no less than four gallons of hair tonic, drop by drop. The demands on his services were so great that he was not permitted to waste time shaving his customers. One sailor spoke of the ship, in the best nautical tradition, as if she were some old flame miserably disfigured before her time. "It breaks my heart to see her now," he said. "Every time I walk through the bar, I can't look."

Life on board a troopship is inevitably monotonous, but soldiers are perhaps better equipped to adapt themselves to it than civilians would be, since a large part of their lives is spent doing the same things over and over again, anyway. Because of space limitations, no sizable drills could be held. From time to time part of a deck would be cleared for calisthenics or for a lecture on some military subject. My company received a number of talks on Australia; they painted a uniformly rosy picture of the continent, since just about the only source material on board was a pamphlet issued by an Australian organization roughly equivalent to an American chamber of commerce. Recreational facilities were no more abundant than those for training. A regimental band traveling with us gave occasional concerts on deck and in the mess hall, and near the end of the voyage there were a couple of variety shows by soldier entertainers. For the most part, however, entertainment was impromptu and consisted largely of group singing in hallway corners, sometimes to the accompaniment of a harmonica or guitar, and card or dice games, which began to flourish before we had left the dock in California and continued until our arrival in Australia. The games were enlivened by the fact that in the middle of the trip each soldier on board was issued five dollars, as effective a morale-builder as a tot of grog. On only one morning, the day we crossed the equator, was the ship wholly given over to conviviality, with the necessary exceptions of the gun crews, the other guards, and the ship's crew. That day, a very hot one, was devoted to the traditional initiation ceremonies for people crossing the equator for the first time. If every man on board who fell into that category had taken his turn at being dunked into a barrel of water, sprayed with a hose, paddled, and subjected to various other forms of good-natured abuse, the ceremonies would have lasted several days and concluded at some latitude remote from the equator. A number of men, therefore, were selected by lot from the units on board to enjoy the experience, while their fellow soldiers looked on observantly, all no doubt planning to write home about the mirthful indignities they had personally endured. A photographer took some snapshots of the events, and when he later offered the prints for sale he received more than three thousand orders. The most popular shot was of a group in which several of the faces were blurred, so that almost any soldier could identify himself as one of the participants.

After a week or so out we no longer took much interest in what day it was, with the result that, when we got to the international date line and lost a full twenty-four hours, nobody cared much except a couple of men deprived of birthdays and a few conscientious company clerks trained to submit daily reports of one kind or another and at a loss how to justify the absence of a day in their otherwise orderly records. On ordinary days, when we lost at most one hour, the soldiers who weren't on guard duty spent their time eating, sleeping, and discussing idly the question of when they might be sailing in the opposite direction, a subject that filled in many a gap between naps and meals. There were two mess halls on board, one for officers and one for enlisted men. We were served cafeteria style, moving with outstretched trays past a line of galley workers, who deftly tossed food at us as they urged us along. We ate in what had once been the first-class dining salon, sitting down wherever we could find an empty place and eating hurriedly, to make room for the soldiers filing in behind us. After leaving the salon and yielding our trays to a crew of dishwashers, we were usually handed an apple, an orange, a pear, or an ice-cream stick. Ice-cream sticks constituted our dessert so often that some of the men, unable to believe that so many of the delicacies could have been loaded on the ship, accepted the explanation of the ship's newspaper that they were manufactured in a refrigeration plant in the hold and enthusiastically signed up for guided tours through the freezing area, where, it was promised, samples would be given away. Actually, of course, ice cream comprised only a small fraction of the thousands of pounds of foodstuffs taken along.

There was some seasickness, but it did not seem to affect the length of the mess line. The Pacific, for one thing, lived up to its name astonishingly well; the only really rough seas we encountered were just off the coasts of California and Australia. Our first day out was our roughest, and despite the fact that fully half the soldiers on board were moderately sick, nearly all of them doggedly tried to get to the mess hall. Soldiers do not like to miss a meal even when they suspect they may not retain it long enough to digest it. On that first, pitch-

ing day the soldiers who did get sick were shy about mention-
ing their malady and generally insisted stoutly that they would
be all right if they could just lie down somewhere for a minute. Someone, browsing through the stocks of the post exchange on the ship, discovered that a tinned variety of lemon
drops was advertised as a cure for unsteady stomachs, and
lemon drops were shortly sold at a rate probably never en-
visioned by the most optimistic of their makers. Until the
supply ran out, a few days before we sighted land, we continued to eat them despite the fact that our stomachs needed
no citric fortification. We had acquired the habit, and as we
sailed smoothly across the South Seas we munched lemon
drops from blackout to blackout.

The lemon drops also came in handy because, as their manufacturers were not reluctant to publicize, either, they were admirable thirst-quenchers. Though not precisely in a position
like that of the Ancient Mariner, we were unquestionably sur-
feited with unpalatable water and short of the fresher variety.
A ship traveling on an extended journey and carrying far more
than its normal complement of passengers cannot hope to load
enough water to meet both the primary demands of drinking
and cooking and the secondary one of washing. We washed,
therefore, in salt water. Occasionally we received a cupful
of fresh water to shave with; usually, however, we shaved
with salt water, as untidy an operation as trying to scrape
tenacious barnacles off a hull. For a while the situation seemed
brighter, an enterprising corporal having discovered that he
could whip up a merry lather by using root beer as a solvent,
but his invention became useless when the post exchange ran

out of root beer, along with Pepsi-Cola and the few other soft
drinks it sold. In addition to these spiritless drinks and to
lemon drops, this canteen was stocked with cigarettes, candy
bars, crackers, sardines, toilet articles, salted peanuts, and
shoestring potatoes. Near the end of the voyage we were
limited to a choice of cheese crackers, potato strings, and cigarettes; finally there was nothing left but cigarettes. They cost
us seventy cents a carton, or two packs for fifteen, a sensational
bargain that was offered as soon as we had left the United
States twelve miles behind.

We had, as a matter of fact, two post exchanges. One, a
rough, soldierly bazaar, was housed in a gloomy corner of the
ship that had once evidently been storage space; the other was
set up rather incongruously in a ladylike gift shop, whose
showcase had been left intact, presumably because it was too
small for a soldier to sleep in. While awaiting our turn there
to shout for candy bars and a tin of lemon drops, we could
stare thoughtfully at glittering cigarette cases, women's hand-
bags, and other trifles designed to gladden the heart of the
feminine half of the mixed-doubles deck-tennis team. Nobody
attempted to buy any of these trinkets or even price them.
They remained where they were throughout the voyage, the
last vestigial traces of the seagoing civilian. The Army had
so completely taken over everything else that even the ship's
crew seemed at times to have become militarized. I over-
heard one steward calling another, whom he considered
derelict in his work, a goldbrick, a term of disapproval usually indulged in only by soldiers.

As our ship zigzagged determinedly toward an undisclosed

port, it occurred to some of us that our voyage in certain respects paralleled that of Columbus. Like his convoy, ours, a group of ships huddled for collective security on a tiny drop of an apparently limitless ocean, was sailing toward what, for practically all its passengers, was a strange and baffling land full of geographical peculiarities and bound to produce new and dangerous adventures. Like the men on the *Santa María* and the *Niña*, the men on our ship were sailing by an uncertain course known only to their captain. How I got to Australia I shall probably never know; we were not told precisely what parts of the Pacific we were crossing, and none of us felt that we were being deprived of any information that was rightfully ours. Soldiers on land or at sea do not have to worry about when or how they are going somewhere, or even where; such matters are out of their hands. They are accustomed to unexpected travel in unpredictable directions and surprised by nothing they encounter. When, near the end of our trip, someone saw a bird flying overhead and remarked that it had perhaps flown from New Zealand, he mentioned the place as matter-of-factly as a year ago he might have spoken of a neighbor's tree.

Our arrival was quiet. The first indications that our trip was coming to an end, aside from the bird and the faint, abnormal sight of land, were that we were permitted to relinquish our lifebelts and that everyone began moving around in a restless hustle doing commonplace errands with remarkable zeal. When, finally, we docked, there were no crowds to meet us. Jammed together along the deck rails, we exchanged pleasantries with a handful of Australians on the wharf and hurled a barrage of whistles at a few girls who walked by. Some of the soldiers threw cigarettes to the girls. Other soldiers threw cigarette butts into the water, happy in the knowledge that the refuse would be viewed only by friendly spotters. A few Australian soldiers boarded the ship and immediately began exchanging souvenirs with us, gratefully accepting, in return for tokens from Tobruk and Greece, superfluous bits of American apparel and insignia. We stayed on the ship for a couple of days while it was being unloaded. The first time I got off the boat, I was with about fifty other men. We were immediately marched off behind a warehouse for a half-hour's close-order drill. Except for the fact that our legs felt a little strange on a solid foundation, it was just like doing close-order drill back in the United States. We felt at home.

2

But Where Are the Kangaroos?

MANY of the soldiers in our expeditionary force arrived at Australia expecting to be met at a primitive wharf by aborigine porters on kangaroos. This misconception existed because, in many of the conversations we held while approaching, we had dwelt on its more unusual features, talking expectantly of boomerangs, platypuses, and the like, and never bothering to take into serious consideration the possibility that we might encounter a substantially familiar civilization, even if spelled "civilisation." In the light of these anticipations, some of the men's first impressions were rather anticlimactic. The pier at which we drew up would have passed muster in any self-respecting American seaport and it was populated wholly by fully clad white officials riding around prosaically in motor vehicles. Some of the cars, to be sure, were propelled by charcoal burners lashed to their bumpers or running boards, but this wartime exigency wasn't particularly startling to us, since, even from the meager reports we had received of events back home, it seemed not unlikely that some New Yorkers were using charcoal burners, too.

Our first Australian acquaintances were a few of the local

soldiers—who, we soon learned, should informally be called "diggers"—stationed at the dock to help us unload. They were so affable and so eager to exchange souvenirs that we were embarrassed, feeling that we should have more fully provisioned ourselves with tradable trinkets. They marveled at the amount and variety of our equipment, asked us how much we got paid, and told us the current price of beer in their community, one of the larger Australian cities. We gathered around them and egged them on to talk, enchanted by their strange, occasionally incomprehensible manner of speech. Australians, though separated by thousands of miles from their mother country, show a blithe, imperial disregard for the tonal qualities of vowels. One of the diggers had a local newspaper with him and left it on board. It was an eight-page edition printed in small type, conservation of space obviously being among its editorial policies. The lead story was printed on the upper left, rather than the upper right, corner of the front page, perhaps in keeping with the British custom of driving on the left side of the road. The paper hospitably carried several paragraphs of news under the head of HOME NEWS FOR U. S. FORCES, a department that catholically contained not only production reports from American armament factories and baseball scores but also such home news as the fact that a total of three hundred frogs had been entered in an annual frog-jumping event in California. From the rest of the paper I judged that Australia's war effort did not allow for the matching of talented frogs. Almost the entire paper was devoted to war news. There was a column of memorial notices inserted by families of Australian sol-

diers. We learned from it that the Australian abbreviation for
private is not "pvt" but "pte." We learned from other sections
of the paper that partial blackouts, nightly occurrences
throughout much of the continent, were called brownouts and
that families inserting birth notices almost invariably referred
to an arriving girl as "a bonny daughter" and usually rendered public tribute to the doctors and hospital staffs who
assisted in the delivery of a child of either sex. The advertise-
ments indicated that the amount of each item the shops could
sell was restricted and that their quotas were generally exhausted within an hour or two of their opening their doors.
One department store announced solemnly that the visit of a
distinguished corset fitter to its premises would be her last for
the duration. Perhaps the day of our convoy's arrival will be
remembered by Australian women with intractable figures
as the beginning of the end.

We were the first American troops to land at what we were
all carefully advised to start calling "Somewhere in Australia,"
a geographical evasion which, after you have inscribed it at
the head of several letters home, makes you begin to feel like
a character in a communiqué. Because we were a novelty and
at the same time a kind of sea-borne manna, we were received
with both curiosity and affection. We were quartered at an
Australian Army camp in a pleasant rural setting, and local
press photographers, though not permitted to disclose our
precise location, called on us at once and took numerous pictures which were published over guarded but enthusiastic
captions. The newspapers ran charts of our insignia to prevent civilians from inadvertently insulting a master sergeant

by referring to him as a private first class, along with feature stories telling how we reacted to Australian customs and Australian coffee, to the second of which our reaction was often unquotably unsympathetic. The reporters who came out to visit us seemed disappointed on the whole that their country didn't strike us as being especially strange, and they brightened perceptibly whenever a soldier asked them how long it would be before he saw his first kangaroo.

Since, of course, the seasons in Australia are reversed, winter begins in June, and it was quite cold when we arrived at our tin-sided, unheated barracks, called "huts." Upon reaching a new location, soldiers immediately look for a place to eat and a place to sleep. We trooped hungrily into a mess hall even before we had examined our barracks, and stuffed ourselves with Australian cheese, which some boys who came from Wisconsin graciously acknowledged to be nearly the equal of the home product. Then we dug up some burlap sacks, carried them over to a haystack conveniently situated only a few hundred yards from our huts, and made ourselves some serviceable, if lumpy, mattresses. We were all settled. A short while afterward our infantry columns began marching out into the countryside on conditioning hikes to harden up leg muscles slackened by inactivity at sea, and our jeeps clattered up the roads, the drivers swerving self-consciously as they suddenly remembered that they were driving on the wrong side.

We began to realize how far from home we were when we found out that none of the movies playing at the camp theater, which featured American pictures, were less than a year old.

Most of us had seen the pictures, but so long ago that we had forgotten what they were all about and were perfectly willing to be re-enlightened. The first time I went to the theater, the picture showing was *Buck Privates*, Abbott and Costello's earliest invasion of the military sphere. I had forgotten what a delectably fictional slice of camp life it depicted, with lovely hostesses assigned to every service club and the Andrews Sisters on hand to hum juke-box favorites at the drop of an overseas cap. Some Australian soldiers in the audience, dumfounded by the revelations on the screen, muttered enviously that our lives in camps back home must have been sybaritic indeed. Their confusion was nothing, however, compared to that of many American soldiers at the end of the show. They stood up respectfully upon hearing the first chords of what they assumed was *America* and were taken aback to find the music illustrated on the screen by a picture of George VI. A couple of Australian soldiers whispered informatively, "*God Save the King.*" Complete international order was thereupon established with the playing of *The Star-Spangled Banner*, appropriately accompanied by the faces, in succession, of General MacArthur and President Roosevelt.

We spent most of the off hours we had in camp hanging around the barracks or patronizing Australian canteens, which, until our own opened up to sell the stocks we had brought with us, did a thriving business among the Americans, who made their first purchases out of curiosity and then kept coming back for more. The Australian sergeants working behind the counters were staggered by the Americans' demand and capacity for milk, which cost only threepence, or a little less than a nickel, for a sizable bottle. In the temporary absence of Coca-Cola and other soft drinks we had grown up on, we turned to ginger beer and lemon or orange squash, sold for sixpence in quart bottles with rubber stoppers. Our favorites among all the Australian delicacies were meat pasties, which, once we had determined that they were not typographical errors, we accepted as tasty local versions of chop suey, enveloped in pie crust. Many soldiers, after making a purchase, on their first trips to the Australian canteens, would simply extend a handful of Australian coins they had previously received as change for American bills and trustingly invite the countermen to remove as much as they wanted. It didn't take the soldiers long, however, to become thoroughly acquainted with Australian currency and aware of their proper obligations to the last ha'penny. American currency practically went out of circulation. We received our wages (including a twenty per cent bonus for being on overseas service) in Australian money, and in the gambling that inevitably followed this disbursement it soon became apparent that the era of the quarter as the standard unit in military games of chance was over. It had been supplanted by the florin, a coin of approximately the same size, worth two shillings, or about thirty-three cents. This departure from the norm was received without complaint by all except the losers, who soon found to their dismay that each time they dropped six florins at the pace with which they would formerly have squandered half a dozen quarters, they were out not a dollar and a half but two dollars.

If the Australians influenced our lives by imposing their

monetary system upon us, we influenced theirs, too. Not long
after we had disembarked, one of the daily newspapers in
our vicinity carried an advertisement for a medicated skin
soap in which a young lady, whose complexion, from one
photograph to another, had miraculously improved, was being
complimented thereupon by a young man. "Say, honey," he
was exclaiming, "even in the States they don't come prettier
than you!" Like most of the male models in contemporary
Australian advertising—and like most of the males in Australia today—he was wearing a uniform, in this particular
case the uniform of an American technical sergeant.

Australian women do not differ from American ones in
their susceptibility to flattery, but they seemed far more interested in the companionship of the American soldier, and
on first becoming acquainted constantly contrived to remove
buttons from his uniform as remembrances. Dances were frequently held in the towns near our camp, and a considerable
number of the girls who attended them showed up in evening dresses. This formal touch, we learned, signified merely
that the Australian ladies did not want to be seen dancing in
cotton stockings or no stockings. They can't get silk, but they
aren't grumbling, of course, as long as they aren't visited by
the people who grow it.

The hospitality of some Australians toward the American
soldier was extraordinary. They seemed to consider it an
honor to entertain us in their homes and to greet us cordially on
the streets. One soldier, who in the United States had never
known the pleasures of fame, was agreeably astonished when,
on walking down an avenue in a near-by town, three small

boys separately approached him and requested his autograph. Whenever we received passes and went into town, we usually ran into some civilians who wanted to be kind to us. A middle-aged lady, getting off a train at the same station with a friend of mine and myself, asked us where we were going, and when we said we were planning to walk to our camp, twelve miles away, unless someone came by and gave us a lift, she insisted that we come to her house first. "Can't leave without a spot of tea, y'know," she said. She proceeded to give us a spot of tea, meat pasties, cake, bread, and jam, and to ask us to come and stay at her place whenever we were around and in need of a bed. She had two sons in Syria.

At the end of our first month in Australia, none of us had seen a kangaroo except a couple of soldiers who had gone to a zoo and inspected one sulking in a cage. We hadn't seen any aborigines or boomerangs or platypuses, either, and had concluded that this continent was a normal, satisfactory one, though in an absurdly out-of-the-way spot for mail service from home. All in all, we were probably no more disappointed at not finding the unnatural wonders we had anticipated than an Australian soldier would be on going to the States, walking into a saloon, and not finding a single customer in a ten-gallon hat shooting his girl's initials into the bar mirror.

3

All In Down Under

PEOPLE visiting a strange land are apt to take most notice of what seem to them its abnormalities, and thus we American troops stationed in Australia began to observe with special delight such preposterous facts as that the local citizens insisted on saying "all in" when they meant "all out," that places prominently identified as bars sell milk and a saloon is a hairdresser's, that a recent Christmas was spoken of by the weather-minded folk among them as one of the hottest days on record, and that taxi drivers were enjoying a remarkable prosperity in spite of a stringent rationing of gasoline, called, contrarily, petrol. Although we could claim no credit for having affected the Australian vocabulary or the Australian climate, we contributed substantially to the happiness of the cabmen, whom we would commandeer at sizable fees to ferry us back to our camps when our occasional brief leaves expired. Civilians who would have liked to ride home after an evening out found it almost impossible to pick up a cab, or even reserve one hours in advance. The average taxi driver, unwilling to expend any of his meager ration of petrol on a short and only mildly profitable haul, preferred to wait for

American soldiers who were approaching the end of their allotted time, hovering near them like a rather mercenary fairy godmother looking after Cinderella.

Once America troops ceased being a rarity in the particular sector of the continent I was first in, the citizenry slowly became accustomed to our ways. Our presence had a profound effect not only on transportation but also on smaller-scale activities. The newspapers ran pictures of Australian girls diligently sewing stars on American flags, for which the demand markedly increased, and one delicatessen store, making an all-in drive for American trade, proudly posted a placard announcing that it stood ready to serve triple-decker sandwiches, Yankee style. Up to then, Australian delicatessen workers had seldom seen any reason for employing more than two slices of bread in the manufacture of a sandwich, but they were willing to cater to our peculiar whims. The American soldier in Australia could afford the loftiest sandwiches conceivable. Congress had thoughtfully boosted our pay, and there wasn't a single one of us whose salary was less than sixty dollars a month. Impeded by low Australian prices and vast Australian hospitality, we found it difficult to spend all we earned, with the result that many soldiers, for the first time in the history of civilized warfare, reached payday with the astonishing realization that they were not totally broke. A growing list of rationed consumers' goods (we had no cards for a while and thus couldn't buy these) also contributed to our affluence. The best hotel bars matter-of-factly sold a one-ounce portion of Scotch for a shilling, or about sixteen and a half cents, a price a New York hotel would hardly quote even to a convention. In many hotels, incidentally, the bars were tended by gentle old ladies of grandmotherly mien, who replied sternly, in answer to a transient's supposition that they were stand-ins for men on battlefields, that they had been bartending for a good long time and regarded theirs as an honorable and dignified profession. When an American told one of them that in his neighborhood at home bartenders frequently kept sawed-off baseball bats under the counters, implements ladies such as she would clearly never dream of wielding, she shook her head wonderingly and said that this confirmed her worst opinion of the United States.

American soldiers, hoping to relieve their bulging pockets of accumulated wealth, were foiled in this aim most often, perhaps, by the generosity of the Australians, some of whom seemed offended whenever we paid for something they could give us. Their homes were so wide-open to us that it is doubtful whether an American housebreaker would have been suspected in the more hospitable areas unless he publicly announced the mischievous nature of his visit. I entered one home, legally, one afternoon and was so graciously received by its household that I felt for a moment they must have mistaken me, noncommissioned as I was, for a lieutenant (pronounced, of course, "leftenant," to the great satisfaction of all American officers authorized to respond to that elegant title). Like many other Australians, the family insisted, at the close of a rather stupendous meal modestly called tea, that I take a second cup of tea, even though their quota for the week was already nearly exhausted. The father of the house was an in-

surance salesman now serving as a staff sergeant in the Australian Militia Force—the Home Guard, as distinct from the
Australian Imperial Force or overseas troops. (Australians, as
fond of the alphabet as we are, invariably refer to these groups
as the A.M.F. and the A.I.F.) His younger son, a boy of four-
teen, had taken to collecting American coins and was disturbed when I failed to have on my person a fifty-cent piece,
the only gem missing from his hoard. The elder son, a lad
nearing eighteen, was eagerly awaiting his birthday so that
he could follow his father into the A.M.F., the A.I.F. being
restricted to full-grown men of nineteen or more. He was a
student at a university and told me, without indicating he
thought there was anything spectacular about his curriculum,
that he had already studied German, French, Spanish, Russian, Chinese, and Malay, and would, by joining up, be pre-
vented from tackling Japanese and Hindustani. His mother,
whose father some seventy years ago emigrated from Phila-
delphia and endowed her with a feeling of kinship toward all
Americans, told me she was so happy I had happened to be
passing by their house around teatime. (Her polyglot son
had seen me walking by and had come running down the
front steps to ask me, in English, to drop in.) She explained
that the whole family had been fretting for a number of weeks
because, while all their neighbors had had an opportunity
to entertain chance Americans, somehow or other she had
never before corralled one. "I've had bad luck all along," she
said. "I never even got any Australian soldiers. They told me
ten weeks ago I could billet some here, but after we got all

set they never came. Everybody else got soldiers, and I'd have been left out completely except thanks to you."

Being in an Australian home had numerous advantages over being on an Australian street, at least in the nighttime. The street was likely to be dark, gloomy, and practically devoid of cars. This absence of heavy vehicular traffic at almost any hour caused trouble for Americans, who blithely started to cross streets regardless of signals and were peremptorily stopped by Australian bobbies, resolved that no one should profane the sanctity of a red light. At night, even the few buildings that were open to the public were so screened and shuttered, because of the partial blackout, that it was possible for a visitor, invited, say, to a dance, to walk by the building where it was being held without guessing that things were proceeding merrily within. Many dances were held for our troops, and the Australian girls seemed to take more eagerly to the shag than Americans did to a curious shuffling glide favored there. A swing band mustered from the personnel of the outfit I was in achieved enormous popularity, and almost singlehandedly introduced to the Australians American's newest hit tunes. Australians, though fond of jazz, become acquainted with our favorites so long after they have come and gone at home that shortly after we got there we were unable to figure out whether a vogue for *Alexander's Ragtime Band* was traceable to the original publication of the song or to its appearance in a movie a couple of years ago. On the other hand, the comparatively new play, *The Man Who Came to Dinner*, was already enjoying a decent run on this continent, despite the audiences' evident inability to understand many of its Bucks County epigrams and despite the fact that one of its actors, a gentleman playing a character universally accepted by Broadway critics as a facsimile of Harpo Marx, seemed, by both his make-up and a thick Italian accent superimposed on his Australian inflection, to be trying to assume the characteristics of Chico.

The American troops became thoroughly accustomed to Australian food, which consisted mainly of mutton, a dish that appeared so persistently in our lives that it seemed to be gradually usurping the staff functions traditionally assigned to bread. One bit of table talk favored in all our messes was a bitter lament to the effect that the mutton might not have been so bad if only they'd sheared the sheep more closely before cooking it. Soldiers in town, able to select their own entrees, were partial to steak and eggs, an Australian specialty, and ordered with the same eager regularity with which they used to ask for steak unadorned. Although perfectly willing to serve eggs with steak, Australian restaurateurs, as well as the waitresses who front for them, were reluctant to humor the Americans, who, for some fool Yankee notion, liked to complement their sirloins with salads. On two occasions my attempts to obtain this combination created furors in respectable cafés. The first time, the waitress thought I was joking and, when I repeated this absurd demand without wavering, went off muttering. She later brought the steak, artfully planted in the center of a huge dish and surrounded by symmetrical fragments of pickled beets. The second time,

the waitress jotted down my order and walked away from
the table, to the dismay of a companion of mine who was
just about to reveal his choice. When we got her back and
asked why she hadn't taken his order, she pointed to me and
said, "Why, I thought he'd ordered for both of you."

When you get halfway around the world from home, the
receipt of a letter assumes the utmost importance. Our first
shipments of mail were delightful and full of surprises. The
second-class mail we hoped we had left behind us had pur-
sued us doggedly, possibly in bottles. Magazines and newspapers that evidently had chased us in vain all over the
United States finally caught up with us, ragged at the edges
but still satisfyingly legible. No matter how much first-class
mail we got, we always felt that it wasn't enough and that
the most affectionate missives were at the bottom of the
ocean. Soldiers with notably durable correspondents often
reaped as many as twenty letters from one of them at a time,
creating great confusion in cases where the writer back home
had innocently dated the messages simply "Thursday."
Though we seldom got letters in the order in which they
were written, and though days without mail were as plentiful
as sheep, we were impressed with the efficiency of the Army's
postal service, especially when it came to the handling of
V-mail. After our eyes got used to those tiny, glossy photo-
static replicas of letters, we accepted them grudgingly, though
they weren't exactly like the real thing. By the time impas-
sioned sentiments have been photographed and printed in
miniature, they have acquired a distressingly documentary
air, and some correspondents who surmised, while writing,

that their cryptic script would perhaps be illegible when re-
duced to a fraction of its size were quite right. But, large or
small, the mails did get through.

Perhaps the record for a well-traveled letter belongs to a
Mother's Day card sent to an American lady in care of her
son, an officer with our troops. It had been mailed originally
by his brother in Alaska, had proceeded determinedly to
Massachusetts, doubled back westward, and arrived in Australia ten thousand miles from its intended recipient and a
considerable time after Mother's Day. The officer put it into a
fresh envelope and sent it back to the United States, enclos-
ing a note to his mother saying that, although, as an occasional message, the greeting was somewhat outdated, it would
at least have achieved the formidable distinction of having
traveled thirty-three thousand miles. Hearing about that, it
occurred to some of the rest of us that we wouldn't be surprised if, before we got back to our mothers, we made that
figure look like chicken feed.

4

Waiting

AMONG a batch of letters I received from home several months after arriving in Australia were two from my mother, each accompanied by a newspaper photograph showing American troops crowding the decks of an Army transport as it docked in some distant Pacific port. Both pictures were garnished with arrows pointing to a tiny, blurred figure which my mother had judged, evidently purely by maternal instinct, to be me. It happened that each time she had the wrong ship, but the care with which she must have scrutinized the pictures gave me some idea of how excited the families of the men in my outfit were at our presence down under, and how diligently they filtered the news for any shreds of information that, by vigorous exercise of the imagination, might be held to apply to us. It was comforting to know that their attitude justified the observations of the popular song writers—that, though gone, we were not forgotten—but we were somewhat surprised that our families still regarded with wonder the circumstance that we were stationed in that particular sector. We had grown used to being here, and no longer considered it odd that we were separated from our homes by such outlandish barriers as the Fiji Islands, which, in our new concept of geography, were merely a small fraction of a vast part of the world that the war had transferred from our West into our East.

There were other bits of evidence of the effect our being overseas was having at home. An Australian periodical, for instance, republished a poem Eugene Kinkead, the poet, wrote for an American magazine—an appeal to the laughing kingfisher, a South Seas bird reputedly given to harassing sleeping soldiers by fits of avian mirth. We much appreciated, from a literary point of view, Mr. Kinkead's thoughtful plea that any kingfishers near our camps should refrain from hilarity during our slumbers. It would have taken more than a bird of even the most flagrant risibility, however, to disturb our sleep. It took, in fact, a laughing sergeant with an astonishingly large pair of hands, who got up a half-hour or so ahead of the rest of us and, at reveille, roamed relentlessly from cot to cot, chuckling to himself and tugging at the limbs of soldiers less heroically proportioned.

Like troops everywhere, we indulged in a good deal of horseplay, beginning with the arrival of our sergeant in the morning and going right on until we were once more cradled under the Southern Cross, a leading local constellation not to be confused, as we old-timers soon learned, with the false Southern Cross. Any soldier moving into the barracks, though regarded for the first couple of hours as coldly and impersonally as if he were a novitiate at the Harvard Club, settled into the swing of things in no time at all, and even before he knew the nicknames of his new buddies, he addressed

them with the contempt we invariably used to denote fa-
miliarity. The married men among us became reconciled
to the constant slandering of their languishing wives at home,
and paid practically no attention to remarks that in more
peaceful days would have evoked husbandly wrath. After
we had been in Australia for a decent interval, a few soldiers
acquired either wives or sweethearts, and along with them, a
share of the heckling. International marriages were frowned
upon by the Army; a man had to obtain consent not only from
the girl's family but from his commanding officer as well.
Many of us became well acquainted with Australians of both
sexes and all ages, and for the most part the people were so
generous to us that one private, for example, reading in the
paper of the death of an Australian businessman who had
often entertained him at his home, applied to his company
commander for a pass in order to attend the funeral. "I felt
that I was one of the family," he said. "I called him Pop."

When we were not at work or visiting our new friends, we
hung around our quarters, playing cards, writing letters,
cleaning and repairing our equipment, and arguing inter-
minably about the relative merits of our home states, coun-
ties, cities, and side streets. One soldier, most of whose pay
was allotted to his wife, devoted many of these off hours to
regaining solvency by sewing on chevrons for men who had
been promoted since coming overseas. He did such a thriving
business that he even tried to buy a portable sewing machine,
an item which, he found, was no longer obtainable. Buying
anything in Australia was, of course, difficult, even with
coupon books. Rationing of petrol and tea had been in effect

for some time, and there were also restrictions on the purchase of clothing. My buddies and I were surprised, and touched, at being given booklets which contained twenty-five clothing coupons and entitled us to make such private purchases as we felt were necessary to supplement our G. I. wardrobes. We weren't quite sure how much the coupons allowed us until one adventurous fellow went off on a buying spree and returned with four pairs of plain white cotton underdrawers, each of which, he reported, represented six of his coupons. He planned to save the one remaining coupon as a souvenir of the war, along with an Australian brooch in the shape of a little boomerang and a letter he received from his family two months after he arrived, saying that they were under the impression he was in England.

We soldiers who suspected that we would eventually be called upon to help propel the Japs back where they came from were on the whole rather proud to be in a theater of operations, though we never admitted it to one another and rarely to ourselves. We were so far away from home that the minor inconveniences of Army life, like wondering when the next furlough was coming, no longer bothered us. Our idea of a lucky soldier was one from New York who was stationed no farther away than Portland, Oregon, with, accordingly, a reasonably good chance of getting back home in a comparatively short time. Knowing that we wouldn't get back to what we hoped would be our ultimate destination for a long time and that there was a good deal to be done before that eventful day would arrive, many of us were eager to get into action as soon as possible. We had read in the papers

the opinions of editorial writers at home who seemed to feel
that our sector was relatively insignificant and that our priority
rating on essential goods of war should have been lowered.
The bombings of Australian ports made it clear to us, however, that the Japs had not noticeably forgotten the continent
we were on, and the sortie of our brothers-in-arms into the
Solomon Islands made us happily aware that our strategists
hadn't forgotten the Japs. We didn't know then where or
when our outfits would be called upon to move into action,
but we had perhaps more reason than most readers of public
statements to remember that General MacArthur had firmly
and repeatedly expressed his resolve to start a large-scale
offensive, and we knew we wouldn't be sorry if, whenever
he called for one, we were it.

5

Change of Gauge

EVEN in the comparatively peaceful days, early in 1940, before Australia first sent its troops far off to take part in a war that was to be waged increasingly closer to their own shores, it was difficult for the average citizen down under to travel any considerable distance by rail without stopping every now and then to switch trains at a change-of-gauge station. Sydney, Melbourne, Adelaide, Brisbane, and Perth, the five largest cities, are also the capitals of five pretty much self-governed states, and it is one of the peculiarities of these proud and individualistic segments of the commonwealth that they look unfavorably upon the width of their neighbors' railroad tracks. Apparently each would be perfectly willing to adopt a uniform gauge, provided, of course, that the other states made the necessary alterations. In recent months Australian civilians have had little cause to worry about changing trains. It is practically impossible for them to do any interstate traveling whatever, unless they can convince the authorities who decide on such matters that their proposed excursion is essential. One Australian girl, who by the exercise of her considerable charm got permission to entrain for a place where she had a date to marry a soldier, was unable to wangle the additional permission for her father to accompany her, the official view evidently being that in these critical times brides haven't the right to be particular about who gives them away.

As a matter of fact, to judge from one wedding in which I became unexpectedly involved, a girl separated by any Australian distance from her fiancé is lucky if she can manage to get to her wedding at all. This particular case involved a sergeant in my company who, after getting the consent of his general to proceed with his wedding, had to surmount further obstacles that made the puny attempts of Hercules to attain his particular goals seem laughable. The soldier met a girl, fell in love with her, and, being the conservative type, resolved to wait for three months before taking the final solemn step. By the end of that interval he was stationed fifteen hundred miles away from her. Suspecting that he was soon going to New Guinea, he sent the young lady several urgent telegrams, instructing her to apply for travel priorities at once, but, because the communications system is run by elves, he didn't receive any reply until the day before he actually pulled out. At that point there was nothing for him to do but wire again and tell her to forget about it. This message reached her just as she was about to step on a train with a bagful of new clothes. A couple of months later, he happened to be stricken with appendicitis and was evacuated back to Australia. As soon as he could, he got a sick leave and, with much difficulty, negotiated the fifteen hundred miles to where his fiancée lived. There he discovered that in order to get married it would be necessary to make a formal announcement of his intentions three days in advance of the ceremony. He had only two and a half days. At the end of that period, he left, still unmarried. A month later, the girl started off again and managed to catch up with him in time to schedule a wedding. It was held, all right, but, on account of a measles quarantine, none of the expected guests could attend. I was the only soldier the groom knew who didn't happen to be affected by the quarantine, and was accordingly pressed into service as the best man an hour before the ceremony. Both bride and groom were rather nervous, possibly because they were conditioned to expect that something would go wrong, and, when the minister asked if anyone had objections, I thought that the bride was looking at me apprehensively, though why she should have I didn't know, since she had never seen me before in her life. As things worked out, she was never even introduced to me until after I had kissed her at the end of the ceremony. When it became evident to all of us that the couple was finally and indisputably wed, there was a violent flood of congratulations, both of the kind normally extended to a bridal couple and also of the kind extended to the winners of marathon dances. A couple of hours later I packed them off on a train, which, in the best local tradition, was guaranteed to make thirty miles in approximately two hours.

During my stay in Australia I made a couple of long trips by rail. On the first I made the acquaintance of several conductors, all of them either women or elderly men who looked as if they were trying to qualify for a second gold watch given to loyal employees with fifty years' service. My longest trip

was on a troop train, and on this there were no conductors
at all, unless you'd count our own officers and noncoms assigned to keep order. Since we had no idea how or when we
would be fed en route, or if, we boarded the train lurching
under the weight not only of our ordinary equipment but of
fruit juices, candy, crackers, tinned meats, and other nourish-
ing impedimenta. It turned out that these, though tasty, were
unnecessary. We were fed, with amazing efficiency, by strong-
armed groups of women at a number of towns along the way.
The women, who had taken over the station barrooms and
restaurants and converted them into huge cafeterias, were
able to serve hundreds of meals in the half-hour or so that
we stopped. We were indescribably pleased when we found,
at one breakfast, that we were to feast on steak and eggs. How
these admirable ladies had been organized into kitchen crews
or how they had become so expert in quick mass feeding we
never found out, but whenever we pulled into a station at
mealtime they were ready for us with sausages and potatoes
and fresh bread and mounds of butter and, inevitably, mugs
of strong tea.

At the stations we spent little time standing still, except
when eating. We took brief strolls along the platforms, pausing to weigh ourselves on penny scales that revealed their
mechanical wisdom, confusingly, in terms of stone. We exchanged pleasantries with young ladies of each town, who
almost invariably asked us to dances the following night, in-
vitations we gravely accepted, though everyone concerned
had good reason to believe we would never see that particular spot again after about ten more minutes. Small barefoot

boys came up to us, too, and asked us to sign autograph books they carried, and officers majestically scribbled their names and full ranks.

On the train there was little to do but play cards and a game of Monopoly someone had brought along, read newspapers and magazines we picked up along the way, and sleep, or try to. We had no berths, so we made the best use of the limited space allotted us. One night a couple of men slept in a passageway, at the suggestion of an Australian officer, who said, referring back, as so many Aussies do these days, to the Middle East campaigns, that he had found it a satisfactory method on the Tel Aviv Express. Perhaps it was, on the Tel Aviv Express, but on the Australian Local our men merely got stepped on and had to return, bruised, to their seats.

Like most soldiers traveling anywhere, we paid relatively little attention to the scenery we passed, even though we were moving through strange areas we might well never see again. There were signs of the war all over: RAAF trainees drilling with bayonets along the tracks, factory workers giving the thumbs-up sign or forming V's with their fingers as we rolled by, and war materials being loaded on flat cars. At one stop, on the outskirts of a village, we were serenaded by some children from a near-by schoolhouse, who, with their teachers, lined up outside our car windows and sang *Waltzing Matilda*, *Bless 'Em All*, and a few other neighborhood favorites. We tossed them candy bars and peanuts, and one grateful soldier threw an apple to a teacher, a young lady who waved a pitchpipe appreciatively as we chugged off.

Shortly after arriving at our new camp, I got to talking to

an Australian lance corporal about the general subject of travel. I remarked that my outfit had moved around a good deal—each time with the many regrets soldiers have at leaving a familiar site and the many doubts they entertain about the merits of an unfamiliar one—and asked him how he felt about the peripatetic life common to all members of our profession. "It doesn't matter to me where I go," he said, "so long as it's north." I asked him if he meant he preferred the northern climate. "No," he said, "I mean toward Tokyo." That was a trip we all, Aussies and Americans alike, hoped to be making soon.

6

First Wallaby

EVEN after you've been in the Army for more than a year, you are still impressed by the way a military organization is able to move into a previously unsettled area and within a relatively few weeks turn it into a place which, if not precisely equipped with all the comforts, can be called home. The second camp in which we stayed in Australia was situated in a wooded section of bushland. It had no streets other than a few dirt roads, no electricity other than that supplied to a handful of headquarters tents by a portable generator, no buildings other than a few mess halls we put up ourselves, no plumbing, no theaters, no churches, no telephone booths, no stores, and none of the hundreds of other conveniences with which a garrison camp back in the States tries to emulate urban life. Nevertheless, this forest community was our home, and we were undoubtedly better prepared than people in gaudier surroundings to fight for it.

Up to the day our trucks rumbled onto our camp site, its only inhabitants were the bizarre beasts, birds, and insects which, according to the naturalists, have been hanging around Australia for many more thousands of years than the fauna

of the other, zoologically less diverting continents. After our
first few weeks there, some of these Australian creatures sul-
lenly retreated into quieter parts, but the majority stood their
ground, no doubt as curious about our intrusion as we were
about their unfamiliar antics in the bush. There are certain
traditionally memorable moments in a man's life—his first
pair of long pants, the first time he kisses a girl, the first time
he shaves, the first time, nowadays, he is bombed. For the
American soldier serving in Australia, there was, in addition,
the first time he saw a wild kangaroo. I never saw any of the
standard variety, the kind that is always insisting on putting
on the gloves, but I saw plenty of giant wallabies, members
of the kangaroo family that are about equal in size to young
police dogs, and no less frisky. My first wallaby passed within
three feet of me, its advent having been shrilly heralded by
the cries of a group of foot soldiers who were pursuing it
through the woods. One of them had been chasing the animal
for five miles, running most of the way. As for my sensations,
I can only report that I felt appropriately incredulous and
giddy.

After we had been there awhile, most of the wallabies
withdrew from the area, perhaps overcome by exhaustion.
The woods, though, remained full of strange sounds and
shapes, moderately alarming by day and more so by night. We
grew accustomed to the sight of an Australian lizard called
the goanna, which, if photographed against a background
that gave no indication of scale, could be passed off as a
dinosaur. Actually, it measures about four feet from the tip
of its long, quick tongue to the tip of its long, tapering tail.

We were often attended, as we walked through the woods at night, by an Australian opossum, occasionally by a mother opossum carrying a baby opossum in her pouch. Soldiers who, back in the days when shooting was a sport, used to amuse themselves from time to time by seeing if they could tree a raccoon, gathered in excited knots at the base of a trunk to which a koala bear was clinging. A few men caught koalas and attempted to make pets of them, but they had little success because the animals declined to eat anything except a special variety of gum leaf. We did not shoot at any of the animals, however; we were saving our ammunition for more deserving targets. We met up with new kinds of snakes and were inclined to exaggerate these encounters, especially in letters home. One soldier captured an eight-foot carpet snake, cooked it, and sampled it; he announced that its taste was halfway between lobster and rabbit. We ran into numerous spiders and fantastic insects beyond our powers of description, and were not surprised to find, on picking up a water can, a scorpion dozing underneath it. All through the day we were serenaded by birds of various sizes and vocal talents, and every evening at precisely the same moment we heard the opening strains of a raucous symphony by the kookaburras, birds more or less onomatopoeically named. Just as it began to get dark, dozens of kookaburras, which had been holding themselves back all day, would start to bray. They kept such regular hours that I took to checking my watch by the noise, as if I were sitting at home nonchalantly dialing Meridian 7–1212.

Our camp in the woods, except for the menagerie attached

to it, had far more American touches than Australian. Walk
up to a group of men crowded around an improvised post
exchange counter, and you would find them buying not tid-
bits of local origin but the same kinds of candy bars and toilet
articles that they would buy in any drugstore back home.
Pass by a crowd of men gathered at night in a partial clearing,
and you would find them gazing raptly at an American movie.
Enter a tent where a candle or gas lantern was burning, and
you would come upon men reading American magazines and
newspapers, which by then were arriving in a steady stream,
about two months after publication. Or the men would be
writing letters home, trying grimly to fill sheets of paper and
at the same time to avoid the hovering wrath of the censors.
Our censors were impersonal and relentless, and so conscientious in their labors that, having been instructed to beware
of communications phrased in foreign tongues, they once
even deleted from a letter to the parents of a devout Catholic
soldier the innocent passage "Pray for us," which, according
to custom, he had written in Latin. Another time they extracted from an envelope a photograph that had been taken
in North Carolina; the background, the offending soldier was
informed in a reproving note, showed in too clear detail the
Australian countryside. It was not too difficult to think of
subject matter for passable letters when you wrote home only
every week or two, but some of the married soldiers among
us, obligated by fervent promises to send some message to
their wives every night, spent many a frustrated hour of composition. One of them, who happened to pick up a high-

school geography of Australia, had the inspired notion of sending excerpts from this to his wife and, by applying himself diligently to his daily assignment, completed the transmission of eight chapters in a week.

Although as time went on, we naturally became more and more accustomed to the ways of the Australians, we began to see so little of our hosts—being permitted to leave camp only at rare intervals and for brief periods—that it was obvious we'd never be Australianized to the extent our families perhaps imagined we already were. Occasionally, when we went for a week without hearing an Australian accent or seeing an Australian uniform, we would begin to feel that we Americans were the natural inhabitants of this territory and that the others who entered it were the aliens. This was confusing to us, and at times, it would appear that the Australians themselves suffered from the same bewilderment. On one of my infrequent trips to town, I observed the interesting spectacle of an American soldier instructively singing *Apple Blossom Time* to three attentive young Aussies. It was clear from the attitudes of all four of them that the American, if recognized as a transient at all, was regarded by his companions as a missionary successfully bringing light and culture to the heathen. Later on I ran into an Australian private who remarked that he had made a couple of visits to the United States. Our conversation thereupon took a strange turn, in which I asked him for his views on things American. He graciously answered all questions. It was as if I had not been in the States for years and he had just returned from an exploratory tour, despite the fact that we were both perfectly aware that his most recent inspection of an American city more or less familiar to me—New York—had occurred in the fall of 1930.

7

MacArthur and His Men

SEVERAL otherwise wide-awake military historians, I have noticed, do not fully understand that the war down under has been taking place in two entirely separate theaters of operation, the South Pacific and the Southwest Pacific, or, if they do, they manfully conceal it. I have frequently seen these names used interchangeably, whereas actually the regions they describe have as a boundary a line as definite, loosely, as the equator. The South Pacific, to clear this matter up, is an area that includes Guadalcanal and many quieter and less renowned islands, including New Caledonia and New Zealand. It is commanded by Admiral Halsey. The South*west* Pacific, consisting of Australia, New Guinea, and various other islands, belongs to General MacArthur.

When we landed in Australia, we were even a bit confused ourselves about which theater we were in, but we did know that General MacArthur was going to be our boss. He had flown in from the Philippines a couple of months before. When our ship tied up at the dock and we looked around in vain for the General, we began to wonder when we would first see him in person. During all the months I was in the Southwest

Pacific, I saw him just three times, but this was, if not a record, a highly creditable showing. Many of the men in my outfit never had the privilege at all, and some of those who did glimpsed him only through the windows of his car. One of my own views, the first, was of this kind. The General is an easy motorist to spot. Even should you fail to notice the four-starred plate on the front bumper, or the rear plate with USA–1 on it (USA–2 is assigned to Mrs. MacArthur), the car itself, the type of long, high, black limousine that would make a doorman instinctively reach for the red carpet, is arresting. So is its chief passenger. He is the only soldier in the Southwest Pacific—or in the rest of the Pacific, for that matter—who is entitled to wear four stars on each shoulder. Also, he carries an admirably flourishable cane, the gold braid swarming on the brim of his floppy hat would delight the most extravagant musical-comedy costumer, and on formal occasions the upper left side of his blouse is so jammed with ribbons that you can scarcely see the blouse. He is an awesome, dramatic spectacle, and Australian civilians, who after several years of war were used to soldiers of all ranks, never tired of hanging around his car waiting for him to approach and display, as he crossed the sidewalk, his inimitable, strolling magnificence.

The time I got closest to General MacArthur, we had a conversational exchange, if "exchange" is the right term for a fragmentary dialogue in which we each uttered two words, my contribution being a respectful *non sequitur*. I happened to be standing in a corridor of his headquarters one morning talking to another soldier when the General came by. Just as he reached me, he inclined his head and said, "Good morning." I was startled by this personal greeting, and by the time I got around to uttering a faint, irrelevant "Yes, sir," he was a good ten feet beyond me. I have since regained my composure, and when anybody asks me today if I ever talked with MacArthur, I reply, with a casual shrug, "Sure," the inflection implying, "naturally."

My third view of the General was a rather inexclusive one, when he made his first and only visit to a bivouac area I was in. He arrived unheralded, causing an understandable flurry at headquarters and leading a mess sergeant who suspected that the General might honor him by sampling his lunch to dispatch a K.P. to his tent for a clean pair of pants. General MacArthur had a major general with him, who, though of sufficiently impressive rank to have made a moderate commotion all by himself in normal circumstances, went as unnoticed as a conscientious seal juggling a ball in one circus ring while a man is shot out of a cannon in another. When it became known that the General was going to address some of the officers, a crew of signalmen set up a microphone and a couple of amplifiers. MacArthur, disdaining any such artificiality, stood about four feet in front of the mike while talking, thus establishing an intimate atmosphere but making it impossible for any single member of his audience, ranged around him in a reverent semicircle, to hear more than half of his remarks. His speech was extemporaneous, but it was full of the rich, labyrinthine sentences that distinguish his prose. His main point, though, was crisply and pointedly made. He said we'd soon be in action. "And I want each of

you to kill me a Jap," he added. Up to that moment few of
us had guessed that we'd shortly be in a position to comply
with such a request. Less than a month later our first detach-
ments were on the way to New Guinea.

Scattered around MacArthur's headquarters, and throughout his military realm, were handfuls of soldiers from the
Filipino, Dutch, Chinese, and British armies, but his command consisted largely, of course, of Americans and Australians. We Americans bumped into Aussie soldiers all over
the place, especially on sidewalks; even long after we had
accustomed ourselves to driving on the left-hand side of the
road, we had difficulty remembering to keep on the left-hand
side of walks. When we went into action, we fought beside
the Aussies, and that something successful was expected to
materialize from this tactical alliance was indicated by the
appearance of an Australian song called *When the Yanks Go
Home Again*, which showed a confident turn of mind. Some
local music critics held that the song had a secondary mean-
ing, that the Aussies would be glad to see the Yanks go home
not only because our departure would mark the favorable
conclusion of the war but because it would give the diggers
a chance to go out with their girls again.

Our chief social asset, unquestionably, was our novelty.
Our uniforms helped, too. The American soldier has a dress
uniform that he rarely has to use for any primarily military
purpose; the Aussie, poor guy, has none. Unless the Aussie
is a general with red plumage on his lapels, he is limited to
one comparatively drab uniform. His shorts, or his long pants
gathered in at the ankles by abbreviated leggings, are his

work clothes and his play clothes, too, and in the company of handsomely dressed Americans he could hardly be blamed for feeling that the sartorial competition was unfair. Though his restricted wardrobe may have its social disadvantages, there are compensations. The Aussie can carry all his equipment, or gear, on his back. No American soldier burdened with all the changes of clothing he is authorized to possess can transport his impedimenta more than a few unsteady yards. The Aussies were perhaps less envious of our garments, though, than of our quantities of ready-rolled cigarettes, which they always accepted with alacrity and not infrequently besought. They have never admired the taste or cost of their home-manufactured brands, so, when they couldn't get American cigarettes, they rolled their own. Cigarette papers are as common in Australia as at a rodeo.

The Australian soldier is usually thought to be more rugged and easygoing than the American, and to have a lovable disrespect for constituted authority. In battle, as a matter of fact, his discipline is exceptionally high. On leave, his attitude, all in all, is pretty much like that of the lance corporal who fell in alongside me one afternoon as I was walking down a street and, after I had offered him a cigarette, explained that he had no objection to saluting officers while he was on duty but that he would be bloody well damned if he was going to indulge in any such tomfoolery merely because the path toward a pub of his choice and the path toward the pub of some lieutenant's choice happened to cross. If any generalities can be made about Australian soldiers, they are simply the same ones that can be equally applied to Australian civilians, such as the fact that they have not yet come around to adopting many of the so-called refinements of life that Americans take for granted. It has seemingly not occurred to many prosperous Australians, for instance, that an excellent way of adding to the comfort of their homes in a community where mosquitoes abound is to put screens on the windows; they prefer to complain and burn incense. Aussie soldiers do not conform to type any more than American soldiers do. Some appear to be chiefly devoted to drinking beer, and others like to browse around music shops, listening to the dwindling stocks of phonograph records on hand. A great favorite for a while was Bing Crosby's *Silent Night,* which I heard on several gramophones long after even our most belated Christmas packages from home had been delivered. Some Australian soldiers look like bums, and probably are; some look as if they might have titles of nobility, which they do. Some get into fights with Americans or any other convenient opponents, and many more don't. Some read nothing but the accounts of marital misfortunes with which a certain element of the Australian press is fanatically concerned; some subscribe to poetry magazines.

Nearly all of the Aussies, except the very young and the very old, have been in combat. They have paid a heavy price. A year after the disastrous retreat from Malaya—when they were pushed back so fast that many of the European colonials on the way didn't have time to drink up all the whisky they had accumulated in anticipation of a long siege and were obliged reluctantly to pour it down sinks—the Australian papers were still running notices of casualties in that campaign. There are so many veterans of Greece and Bardia and Tobruk around that their presence arouses no excitement. They don't discuss their experiences much, and this reticence had the effect, soon after we Yanks arrived in Australia and long before we ourselves began fighting, of making us seem foolish and naïve, by contrast, in the talks we had with them on military subjects. One evening I was talking to an Australian captain who had just barely managed to escape from Greece, and I asked him whether he had any complaints to make about the American soldiers he had met. "Well," he said, "I take a dim view of the way you blokes keep telling me how bloody tough it was in the Louisiana maneuvers."

8

Moving Up

After having traveled some fifteen thousand miles toward war without running into so much as a false air raid, it was a source of infinite satisfaction to us to learn that we had been ordered to pull out of our training camp and proceed to New Guinea, a place a year before we would unhesitatingly have bet we would never set eyes or foot on. It was no particular shock to us to be going to an area that was so thoroughly a combat zone that the only civilians in it were aborigines; when we were sent to Australia, we were sure that whatever action we would see would not be on that still peaceful continent. We had been in training for a long time and would have felt hurt if, in the selection of troops for combat, we had been neglected. We weren't; we got in early. Our presence in New Guinea marked the first assumption by American infantrymen of their rightful share of an aggressive burden previously shouldered exclusively by the Air Forces, Navy, and Marines. This distinction did not seem to us at the time to be overly impressive; the average soldier, and especially one in New Guinea, would rather be told where he could get a glass of beer than that he is historically significant. The sol-

diers in my unit applauded loudly and approvingly when we
were advised a couple of weeks before we moved that the
big moment was close at hand. However, when we actually
learned that within twenty-four hours we would be heading
toward a spot where we would not only have a chance to kill
some of the enemy but would, in certain inevitable cases, be
killed ourselves, we took the news calmly. Probably the only
real excitement was provided by the revelation that some of
us were going by air. Our reaction was perhaps best indicated by the remark of a sergeant who, in the middle of a
twilight baseball game, had been instructed to go to his tent
and pack for New Guinea. "Damn it," he said to one of his
pals. "It was my turn at bat."

Following our arrival in Australia, when it became obvious
to us that any advances we made from there would certainly
not be south, we had been studying up on the islands to our
north with considerably more interest than the ordinary tour-
ist might display. As a result, we were quite familiar with
New Guinea, a large, conspicuously uncivilized island afford-
ing few opportunities for ballplaying or other subsidiary soldierly pursuits. Since we were all well aware that what little
time we did not devote to the waging of war up there would
surely not be devoted to spending our pay, one of our first
impulses, when we were warned of the peculiar shape of
things to come, was to dispose of nearly all of our cash. One
soldier, who went to see an early detachment of troops em-
bark, suggested to a couple of men that if they had a few
extra pounds still in their pockets he would be glad to try to
cable the stuff home for them. Word got around, and half

an hour later, somewhat dazed by the response to his offer, he walked away bulging with what, when he got around to counting it, turned out to be the Australian equivalent of five thousand dollars, in small bills. We got rid of other things, too. Those of us who were being transported by air were allowed to carry baggage of only a limited weight, and a good deal of that had to be ammunition. We couldn't be sure that our planes wouldn't land right in the middle of a battle-field. Accordingly, we were ready to fight the moment the wheels stopped rolling. We reluctantly turned in to our supply sergeant most of the clothes we had in the past begged so hard to draw from him, and we even presented him with tenderly polished leather belts and other adornments we had bought ourselves. We burned all the old letters we had been holding, or else packed them up for storage in the hope that we would someday be able to reclaim them. After the first planeload of our air-borne detachment took off, other soldiers had to wander around the airport to collect barracks bags full of equipment which, at the last minute, had to be left be-hind. Men and ammunition had the first call, and they were jammed into planes stripped of seats and other nonessential paraphernalia. Three privates who had never been in a plane before found themselves stuffed into the transparent nose of a bomber, where they huddled together, not especially wor-ried about their rather exposed position but embarrassed because they thought they might get airsick. Their last words, on the momentous occasion of their departure, were a mourn-ful lament to the effect that somebody had neglected to equip their uneasy perch with an empty cardboard container.

The plane I was moving up in was scheduled to leave early in the morning, and my fellow passengers and I didn't go to bed the night before. We were too busy trying to decide which of our clothes were necessary, where to put what we were going to take, and how to carry that. We brought along sharp knives, quinine and vitamin tablets, mosquito lotion, sun glasses, canvas water buckets, and other utilitarian odds and ends. As we boarded the ship, the pilot, a young second lieutenant, bade us welcome and obtained a list of our names, just as if we were commercial plane travelers. Instead of asking us for our addresses, however, he took down our army serial numbers. In addition to his copilot, a staff sergeant, the crew consisted of a sergeant who operated the radio and a private who seemed to have no particular function. He rode with us in the cabin, like a steward, but he didn't pass out chewing gum and tomato juice; he was chiefly occupied in reading an old magazine. We laid our rifles and knives in the plane's baggage racks. We unloaded the rifles, so that a sudden jolt wouldn't set them off, and as a further precaution put our helmets on the floor, lest one of them fall out of a rack and bruise a head it had been designed to protect. On the floor there were parachutes and uninflated rubber lifeboats, and out of both, confidently anticipating no other use for them, we fashioned seats. I shared a corner of a rubber boat, as hard and unyielding a couch as ever I occupied. I regret to have to say that I recall little of what may well have been the most eventful flight of my life, because, despite the unfavorable conditions, I slept through most of it.

I fell asleep shortly after we took off, and when I woke up

we were over the water, about ten minutes away from our
destination. We could see the coastline of New Guinea up
ahead of us. Down below, the monotony of the water was
broken by the outlines of submerged reefs. There was a tiny
ship perched on one of them, and at first we took it to be a
recent casualty of the troubled waters of the area. The private
who acted, or didn't act, as our steward looked up from his
magazine long enough to explain that it had been there, un-
dramatically, ever since the last war. We swung over the
coastline and gathered quickly, from the relief map which
we saw beneath us and which expanded in detail as we circled down to meet it, that, just as we had heard, we were
heading for one of the hilliest areas in the world.

When we landed, we were met by Army trucks and taken
to an Aussie camp, where we were to spend our first night
in a combat zone. All along the way, we saw supply dumps,
carefully camouflaged against aerial observation, and other
installations we could readily recognize as being military. We
didn't see any civilians. We had supper, looked with interest
at the foothills of the Owen Stanley Mountains looming in-
vitingly in the distance, took a quinine tablet apiece, hitched
up our mosquito netting, and went to bed.

9

Somewhere in New Guinea

AFTER the thousands of miles we had covered in such relatively glamorous conveyances as trains, steamships, and planes, it was a little bit anticlimactic for us to move into our first bivouac area in New Guinea, prosaically, by truck. The fact that we did not have to walk was probably something to be grateful for, since it is not a land on which civilization has yet made many appreciable inroads, or, for that matter, outroads. The dirt trails we bounced along for weary hours were in much better shape, we were pleased to learn, than they had been before the Japs began to creep across the island. The road we mainly followed was, not so long ago, merely a trail wide enough to accommodate a couple of natives abreast carrying a load of bananas. Today a heavy six-wheel truck can lumber over it without difficulty, but the passengers are not likely to compose testimonials to the roadbed. We rolled up and down some of the countless hills of which New Guinea seems largely to consist, through patches of jungle with vines hanging down to lash at the heads of tourists who forget to duck, through coconut-palm groves and banana plantations, through tall, wavy fields of grass, and past clumps of rubber trees and other vegetation peculiar to that outdoor hothouse.

Although we were riding along what I suppose the natives called a highway, we saw no towns, for the simple reason that New Guinea has almost no towns. The largest settlement we passed was a native village of a half-dozen thatched huts on stilts clustered about a relatively substantial church with an English name over its door. The church, we gathered, had been put up by missionaries, whose influence was frequently observable in those parts. One group of natives chanted as they worked. Their song didn't have any clearly recognizable tune, but every now and then an English phrase or two would crop up in it—the remnants of an old hymn. Some of them knew a little English, others knew none except the words "smoke" and "cigarette," which they used whenever they met a soldier who might conceivably give them one. As we rode past the settlements in our trucks, we tossed cigarettes down to the natives, and they occasionally offered us a coconut in return. Most of them were little boys, often wholly naked, who sometimes indicated that they were not altogether un-accustomed to soldiers by offering us their crude version of a military salute—just like the little boys who used to salute us back home long ago when we marched by them on ma-neuvers.

Though for some reason or other we saw no little girls, we passed plenty of older ones, many of them as becomingly undressed as if they had just finished posing for the *National Geographic*. They were, inevitably, subjected to admiring whistles. Some of them seemed unmoved by these tributes,

but others, on the shy side, retreated modestly behind trees.
A few of the women had tattooed faces, and almost all of the
men had huge heads of hair, fairly close-cropped at the rim
of the skull but flaring out wildly six or seven inches up. We
felt self-conscious about this because, just before taking off
for New Guinea, most of us had had our hair cut extremely
short, in what we then thought would surely be the style in
a notoriously hot climate. There were supposed to be head-
hunters and cannibals all around the region, but the natives
we met at first were very friendly and didn't even hint that
they would have enjoyed eating us. One of them, in fact,
perhaps to assure us of his strictly vegetarian intentions,
chased the truck I was in for several hundred yards in order
to bestow upon us a handful of small, sweet tomatoes he had
just picked. They were quite refreshing and helped to sus-
tain us through a trip so dusty that by the time we arrived at
our destination we were so black that a casual observer might
easily have taken us for a short-haired tribe of natives.

We set up camp on a rubber plantation, a restful and ap-
pealing spot, even though the mail service was irregular. We
were less concerned with the priceless substance inside the
tall gray trees—to which we fastened our clotheslines—than
with the ill-mannered red ants that frolicked on their trunks.
We got used to having insects of various sizes, species, and
stings around us, however, and wouldn't have thought of going to bed without first tucking in the edges of our mosquito
netting. Our bedsteads were made of bamboo poles. Vines,
we found, made an acceptable substitute for springs, and palm
leaves could be turned into an adequate mattress, but a rest-

less sleeper faced the danger of cutting himself on its fringes. We spent a good deal of time in bed, having nothing else to do after dark. In the absence of better qualified entertainers, we sometimes sang ourselves to sleep, using as lullabies ancient numbers on the Hit Parade. We had never heard the tunes then popular at home.

In an area like that the biggest problem, for soldiers or anyone else, was the transport of supplies. It was impossible to get fresh meat or vegetables or butter or milk to us, and therefore almost everything we ate came out of cans. We were afraid we might forget how to wield a steak knife, since hash (sometimes replaced by beans or spaghetti) was our main dish. Our potatoes came canned and dehydrated, our milk and eggs powdered, most of our fruit dried. We had no ice and one night, when the mess sergeant, using some lemons a soldier had picked down the road, stirred up some delicious lukewarm lemonade, we considered it a real treat. Soldiers, as everyone knows, are inordinately fond of eating between meals. Our off-hour nibbling was confined to coconuts. We became reasonably adroit at puncturing them, drinking the milk, and then chewing the meat after cracking them open with the long, sharp knives we bought before leaving Australia—the most valuable pieces of personal equipment we possessed.

Isolated as we were, we naturally heard little news. For a while, until someone found a radio station in the hills not far away, to which we began making daily trips for worldly enlightenment, we were entirely cut off from information about current events, even those taking place in other sectors of the island. Scarcely had the dusty wake of a passing truck died down than the magnificent rumors which soldiers are supremely capable of brewing would begin to flow. At one time or another we were more or less convinced that Russia had invaded Japan, that Turkey, Eire, and Spain had declared war on Germany, that the Japs had withdrawn from the Philippines, and that the Yankees had won that season's World Series. This last bit of misinformation was probably the most annoying, since it resulted in the erroneous settlement of several small bets.

As an urban selectee's military career progresses, he changes gradually from a preponderantly indoor being into a wholly outdoor one. In New Guinea the last characteristics of the former finally vanished. We no longer regarded it as curious or improper to walk entirely nude along a highway, or to bathe in full view of traffic, since the traffic was invariably military and thus presumably shockproof. We did our bathing, as well as our laundry, in a tropical stream near by. We had no diving platforms, but we could grab a vine on the bank and swing ourselves out over the water, just as we had once swung over water on ropes while going through obstacle courses in our training-camp days. The chief difference was that then we were supposed to come to rest on the opposite shore, whereas in New Guinea we would let go in midair and fall happily into the stream. There were said to be some crocodiles in it, but they were at that time as little in evidence as the Japs. Though we hadn't seen any of the enemy, we were suspicious of all rustlings in the woods, many of which appeared to be caused by the only animals outside of hogs I saw the whole time I was in New Guinea. They had the bodies of opossums and the heads of anteaters, and they walked and breathed just about the way we suspected Japanese patrols did. Although we were hoping to run into some Japs as soon as possible, we didn't mind the comparatively peaceful nature of the life we were then leading. It had its minor inconveniences, but after all it was far less risky than the lives a lot of people who enjoyed a few more metropolitan luxuries had been leading in London two years before.

10

Moresby

A COUPLE of years ago I had never heard of Port Moresby. Today I speak of it familiarly and diminutively as "Moresby," just as habitués of Newark sometimes speak of their home state as "Jersey." I cannot remember now exactly when I first heard about Moresby, but I am sure that my high-school geography teacher, a man no more prophetic than he was omniscient, never mentioned the place, perhaps because he had never heard of it, either. Moresby, of course, is one of those spots, like Narvik and Sfax and Vyazma, which in the past two or three years have risen from cartographic obscurity to positions of some prominence. For a long time Moresby was the only Allied base in the Southwest Pacific north of the Australian continent, and in the summer of 1942 it figured conspicuously in the news when the Japanese, after accomplishing the supposedly impossible feat of crossing the Owen Stanleys by foot, bore down to within a discomfortingly few miles of the city limits. When I got to Moresby the following fall, the doctors and other noncombat troops who had been among the handful of Americans there during the enemy's threatening advance were still breathing heavily. It had looked for a while as if the medics and their stronger patients, along with a few engineer and quartermaster troops no more noted for their marksmanship, might be in for some heavy street fighting.

In peacetime Port Moresby was the capital of Papua and as much of a metropolis as New Guinea could boast. It could not have been an especially prepossessing community even then. It is a good deal smaller than Scarsdale, New York, and its numerous mosquitoes pursue the human body with the same desperate resolve with which the Scarsdale commuter pursues a receding train. Moresby is a dry, dusty, dirty town consisting of a few houses, hotels, warehouses, and docks squatting on a hill that rises from a curving harbor. Most of the buildings are made of wood and many of them, today, are rather splintered, after months of being subjected to enemy bombing. None of the buildings are occupied by their original owners. The white population of New Guinea, except for soldiers, was evacuated a long time ago; the houses and hotels have been transformed into military headquarters. The scrubby fields beyond the town, sparsely covered with vegetation and here and there pocked with bomb craters, have been rolled and pounded into airdromes. There are almost always planes in the skies over Moresby, and lately a large majority of them have been, happily, ours.

Most of the troops and supplies that go to New Guinea pass at one time or another through Moresby. It is a busy port; by day and by night American and Australian army trucks ply steadily between the piers and inland areas, loaded

with gasoline, food, equipment, and men, whose initial ela-
tion at arriving in a city rather than a jungle is quickly dimmed
when they learn that the city has about as many recreational
facilities as a guardhouse. I spent three weeks in Moresby,
not long after my arrival on the island, and lived during much
of that fretful period, with two other soldiers, in a small room
of what had been designed as an elegant hotel. The pro-
prietors had never had a chance to furnish it before the war
compelled them to retire from the hotel business and leave
town. The only pieces of furniture in our room, a typical
one, were the cots and chairs we ourselves brought in. There
was a sink in one corner, but the water was turned on only
at unpredictable and inconvenient moments, such as at four
in the morning, when, if not sleeping, we might be down the
road huddled in a slit trench during an alert and certainly
in no mood for washing. Occasionally we could wheedle a
thin, reluctant trickle out of the tap at a more nearly normal
hour, but this was so rare and miraculous a flow that, by the
time we had finished marveling at it, it wasn't there.

Other Americans in the vicinity, who were living cozily in
tents, now and then sneered at us for being luxuriously shel-
tered in a fancy hotel. In vain we pointed out to them that,
although the place had plenty of bathrooms, we were forbidden to use them and had to patronize a latrine a hundred
yards down a side street. In vain we described the ants that
infested our chamber, ants so small that the only kind of
mosquito netting that could have kept them out of our beds
would also have kept out the air. The ants were less of a

nuisance, at that, than the huge rat which would faithfully crawl through the transom every other night and scratch its noisy way around the room.

There were other disadvantages to living in the hotel. For one thing, some of its rooms were occupied by Air Forces personnel, and every day at noon, looking out wistfully from our second-story window, we could watch a mess truck drive up and dish out handsome meals to the airmen. On the other hand, we had to walk half a mile to a mess that was set in an ugly white stucco building called Shangri-la. This nomenclature was right in keeping with a practice, popular in all desolate corners of the world patrolled by our Army, of naming every landmark after the famous landmark that least resembles it. For instance, it is inevitable that wherever two dreary trails cross at some remote outpost, the junction will be marked by a sign proclaiming that it is the intersection of Broadway and Forty-second Street. The only saving grace of this bastard Shangri-la was that in a hut adjacent to it, about the size of an outhouse, a post exchange had been established, where, every two or three days, you could buy a can of fruit if you were sharp about it. There was only one other place in Moresby that could conceivably be called a store. It was a canteen run by the Australian Army on the porch of another hotel. There, if you waited in line, you could buy chewing gum and quart bottles of concentrated fruit juice, a liquid that proved to have an incredible magnetic attraction for the ants. We consumed large quantities of the stuff—orange and lemon and something called lemon-barley were the principal flavors—in our room, mixing it with lukewarm water that we carried back from Shangri-la after lunch. Ice was unobtainable in the hotel, just as it had been on the rubber plantation. The only ice I ever heard of in New Guinea, as a matter of fact, belonged to one proud hospital that was equipped with an electric refrigerator, for medicinal purposes only.

Our hotel room had its points, just the same. One was that it contained reading matter. Its library was not extensive—an old *Reader's Digest* with a couple of pages missing, an older Harvard *Alumni Bulletin*, and three soiled copies of *The New York Times*—but we read and reread them all, skipping nothing, until we could quote sizable passages to each other, if anyone would listen. At that, we fared better, from a literary point of view, than many of our contemporaries in New Guinea, some of whom had nothing to read at all but letters of their own composition. The lucky few who possessed printed matter hung on to it grimly, regardless of its antiquity. One company treasured a copy of *Cosmopolitan* published in 1934; another passed from hand to hand an ancient *True Detective Story* in which one article contained a timely reference to activities of the chief executive of the state of New York, Governor Franklin D. Roosevelt.

There wasn't much in the way of entertainment in Moresby, but that didn't bother our outfit, because we were just passing through. The Australians stationed there didn't seem to mind much, either. They kept themselves enthusiastically engrossed in two-up, a national game that takes no time or skill to learn, since it consists merely of matching coins. One vacant building, half demolished by a bomb, was their favorite arena, and they would gather there for hours on end flipping pennies and excitedly rooting (or barracking, to use their own word) for heads or tails, represented, fittingly, by the emperor and the kangaroo. Occasionally a military band would give a concert, and there were also outdoor movies, held as soon as darkness fell, so that a complete picture could be shown before any Japanese planes that might be on their way arrived. In the event that the Japs showed up early, the show would be peremptorily canceled, and the mixed audience of Yanks and Aussies and natives would scatter toward the hundreds of slit trenches dug all over town.

The natives who hung around Moresby were a good deal more civilized than those we met later in the rural districts. Many of them spoke excellent English and proved to be a distinct disappointment to newly arrived Americans who were seeking traces of the darker ages. One soldier, as soon as he hit town, took his camera into a native settlement and asked an elderly resident to pose. "Certainly," said the native, showing no fear of the little black box. "That'll be two bob, please." Somewhat nettled at this worldly turn of events, the soldier paid the model's fee, halfheartedly took a picture, and started to walk away, pausing only to try out some sign language on another native, who he hoped would be less domesticated. "Got the time, bud?" this one asked.

If it seemed bizarre to us at first to find such urban wild men, we soon grew accustomed to the notion that New Guinea, today, is an illogical land—half primitive, half modernized by war. You could take a stroll in the country one evening and trip over a vine curling across your path; the next evening you could take an equally unexpected header over some deviously planted strands of barbed wire. The heat lightning and the ack-ack would alternate in brightening up the night sky; streams were shared by crocodiles splashing about idly and engineers testing for bacteria content; convoys carrying elaborate equipment shared the dirt highways with natives padding along on bare feet under loads of unripe bananas. The weirdest combination of all was one you could see before almost any meal at Shangri-la: a fierce-looking native boy, with bushy hair, rings in his ears, bracelets on his arms, and a dazzling red skirt draped from his waist, standing patiently in the chow line with a G. I. mess kit clutched expectantly in one aboriginal hand.

11

Somewhere Else in New Guinea

ACCOUNTS of military activities in New Guinea have sometimes emphasized the arresting fact that, because of the density of the jungle which covers so much of the place, soldiers in the bush frequently hear the enemy before they come close enough—seven or eight feet, say—to see him. While waiting to make visibility tests of our own, we American soldiers struck up a passing acquaintance with the Japanese through occasional night air raids, in conformity with the prescribed order of sound before sight. Comparative veterans in New Guinea habitually boasted to newcomers of their ability to distinguish enemy planes from our own by the uneven drone of their motors, and after not so many weeks there the men in my outfit achieved a similar state of confidence, though we took the precaution of making such auditory distinctions from the security of a slit trench, where an error of judgment was least likely to prove mortal.

Of course, in this war there is nothing novel about being in an air raid, but every man's first raid is an event he will remember and, unless rudely discouraged, talk about. My outfit, thoroughly drilled in air-raid etiquette, went through its initial raid calmly enough, but afterward there was a good deal of spirited rivalry on the subject of just whose slit trench or foxhole had been closest to a falling bomb or ack-ack fragment. None of us were frightened, and I will add that the only time I personally felt any real alarm during an alert was late one night when, after three of us had sat for over an hour on the edge of a trench waiting for something to happen, one of the other soldiers and I dozed off. We were awakened by the clutching hands of the third soldier, a relatively wide-awake fellow, who thought he heard the whistle of a descending bomb and grabbed at us on his precipitous way down to cover. We didn't actually wake up completely until we reached the bottom of the trench, apprehensive and rather dirty.

While, whenever the searchlights probed in the sky, we crouched in our trenches hoping that they'd come to rest triumphantly on an enemy bomber and hold him in their crisscrossed beams till the ack-ack gunners got him, we made ideal objectives for the leisurely aim of cruising mosquitoes. The activities of the local mosquitoes seemed to be perfectly synchronized with those of the Japs. The latter would drive us out from beneath the protective nettings we kept over our beds and into the open, where the mosquitoes, with their motors warmed up and turning over softly, had been waiting to take off. After watching New Guinea's natives, who have never heard of citronella, stroll about with naked torsos and an apparent immunity to the mosquito, you get to thinking, while scratching yourself, that the white man's burden is largely entomological.

Ground troops like ourselves, though sometimes annoyed by enemy planes, had the complementary pleasure of watching our own planes soar past in comforting numbers on their way to harass the enemy. There had always been something fine back home about seeing a formation of bombers or fighters zooming overhead; there was something even finer about seeing them when you knew that they were on a combat mission and that within a few hours after their passing overhead they would probably have provided material for the latest American communiqué. When we first saw them flying by, graceful and destructive, we would all look up and yell, "Give 'em a go, Yank!"—a war cry the Aussies sometimes addressed to us. After we got used to them, we would just look up gratefully.

Before we had been in New Guinea long enough to learn what our families and friends back home were thinking about the fact that we were there, we began to suspect that no matter how diligently they might study their geographies, they would never really be convinced that New Guinea, being an island, was much larger than Staten Island or Nantucket. Actually, of course, that huge area is rather in the Greenland or Madagascar class. Since we were practically isolated in the tiny part of the island on which we had pitched our tents, we sometimes found it hard to believe that, viewed from a world perspective, the whole vast tract was merely a dot of land on which a handful of troops from the American pool of man power were peering through vines for a glimpse of an obscure and stealthy enemy.

Although to us New Guinea, naturally enough, was a geographical sphere of overwhelming importance, we were still not entirely unaware of the events taking place in other sectors. At an outdoor movie show one night the applause that greeted the tantalizing and improbable shot of a soldier downing a glass of beer was dwarfed only by that given to a scholarly Russian telling the newsreel cameraman of the determined resistance of his countrymen. We soldiers, normally undemonstrative about matters pertaining to our trade, cheered happily some nights later upon hearing, through the short-wave static, of the heady accomplishments of the British Eighth Army in Africa. The radio was our one source of information about outside events, and it was also a steady source of entertainment. However, much as we appreciated the news summaries and swing sessions and comic skits that were beamed our way, there was one brief statement that somehow appealed to us more than anything else we heard on the broadcasts. That was when the announcer, talking clearly and crisply lest enemy interference or ten thousand miles of potentially disturbing atmosphere dim the vivid content of his speech, would say, "This is the United States of America."

12

Over the Hill

A FRIEND of mine in the United States, having heard that I had been sent from Australia to New Guinea, wrote me a letter from which I gathered that he thought New Guinea was one of the Solomon Islands, and another friend of mine at home, writing with the same geographical abandon, inquired solicitously whether I got back to Australia frequently for week ends. I began to grow more and more doubtful that certain people at home would ever get over the notion that going from Australia to New Guinea was no more difficult than going from Manhattan to Long Island in the days before the Triborough Bridge was built, or that traveling from one point to another in New Guinea wasn't much more of a problem than it would be to make an overland march from, say, Great Neck to Jones Beach.

We soldiers who took part in the campaign against the Japs in that eastern section of New Guinea called Papua were only too distinctly aware that all Papua is divided into two parts, the line of demarcation being the knife-ridged Owen Stanley Mountains. Perhaps it was provincial of us, but we had the feeling that these peaks had assumed a military importance that few others had had since Hannibal glorified the Alps. All the fighting the Americans did against the Japs was on the northern side of the range, and accordingly it was of great interest to any detachment of troops on the southern side to learn that they were going "over the hill," a phrase that has other connotations among soldiers in the States.

My unit pulled out of its camp in southern Papua early one morning, before one of the unbelievably colorful sunrises peculiar to this area had had a chance to impose itself decoratively on the sky and before the mosquitoes had tired of occupying our beds and hummed off to spend the day resting up in their own. We rolled our packs by flashlight and knocked down our tents by guesswork, accomplishing these tasks with only minor accidents. One involved an orderly, who, while closing a trunk, inadvertently but securely locked into it several square yards of a large tent, then disappeared with the key in his pocket, while a half dozen of the rest of us, unaware of all that, were trying hurriedly to disassemble the tent and fold it up. Everybody was very calm about going except one soldier who, a day earlier, had bought forty-eight precious cans of sliced peaches. Determined not to abandon his treasure if he could help it, he was trying, with the superhuman endurance sometimes exhibited by ordinary men during extraordinary crises, to eat them all at one sitting.

It was just beginning to get light when we piled onto trucks and rode out to the airport, where transport planes were waiting for us. We noticed that some of them were planes that had flown us up to the island from Australia. Almost all the transports in the area had names painted on them, and anybody who has ever made a journey on a ship affectionately labeled *Dirty Gertie* or *Foitle Moitle* is not apt to forget her. Though invariably feminine in gender, these planes had far fewer frills about them than their commercial' counterparts in the States. Instead of seats, there were, along each side, metal benches with concave depressions in them at intervals—not, it was painfully obvious, to accommodate a soldier's anatomy but for the benefit of parachute troops, who have to sit on their chute packs while riding. We didn't carry chutes.

We soon took off and headed across country, seemingly losing altitude as we approached the mountains. Actually, of course, the ground was rising up beneath us, and at times, even though we were more than ten thousand feet up, we could see peaks about us on both sides. We reached our destination in less than an hour. If we had had to march through the thick, clinging jungle that formed a solid mass of green beneath us, we'd have been doing well to make the trip in six weeks. From the air the strip on which we landed looked like a small firebreak. It had been cleared by engineers who had gone ahead of us on foot. We circled over it a couple of times and finally came in, roaring down a path cut through the forest and bouncing to a landing on a bumpy, narrow, grassy lane that served as an airport. We unloaded, marched down a trail to the beach a few miles away, and then boarded native outrigger canoes, which were to take us to a trawler anchored in deeper water a couple of hundred yards offshore, which in turn was to move us up the coast a few miles to our new base.

The adventures of the American Army in the hinterland of New Guinea were full of such contrasts between the ancient and the modern as our sudden shift, within a few hours, from a sleek transport plane to a native outrigger. The outrigger there is a hollowed-out log, turned into a reasonably serviceable boat by the addition of, first, a long, slim wooden pole which projects from one side and rests as a support on the surface of the water some eight or ten feet from the hull, and, second, a raftlike platform of braided strips of wood tied together with vines and placed on top of the dugout. When we first saw a fleet of these outlandish craft and realized that we and all our equipment were to travel on them, we were rather skeptical, and kept looking hopefully up and down the coast for something just a bit newer, like a Chris-Craft. Later, when we saw some native boatbuilders digging at a huge log with chisels, we realized that these canoes were 1943 models and what we had taken for a ridiculously archaic means of travel was the most up-to-date the region had to offer.

In the weeks that followed, we came to appreciate the outriggers. Small and slow as they were, they were often the only things we had in which to move up our supplies. I made a five-hour trip up the coast in an outrigger one day to where we had established an advance base in a native village. Four other people took part in this expedition—a lieutenant who had been weakened by a siege of malaria and as a result became seasick and fell into a deep sleep punctuated only by

an unconscious determination to slide off the raft into the water, where there were supposed to be sharks that would have
been delighted to have him join them; and three native paddlers, two of whom spoke no English at all. The third, a comparative scholar, could understand simple commands and had
a vocabulary consisting of "O.K." and "Thank you," which
he used in alternation every chance he got. He broke up his
repeated professions of assent and gratitude by a plaintive
chant that bore no resemblance whatever to *O Sole mio.*

Next to grabbing the lieutenant whenever he seemed dis-
posed to tumble overboard, my chief duty was to keep our
outrigger upright. Outrigger poles, though ostensibly attached to steady the native craft, seem remarkably unstable
themselves, since the slightest inadvertent motion of anyone
aboard one of these canoes very nearly capsizes it. In order
to maintain them on an even keel, assuming they have keels,
it is necessary to rearrange everything and everyone from
time to time, depending on the direction of the wind and
other variable factors. Our craft was occupied not only by the
lieutenant, myself, and the paddlers but by a number of heavy
cases of ammunition, which were too heavy to shove back and
forth. It therefore fell upon me to squirm sideways whenever we appeared in danger of foundering, which was most
of the time. The greatest single threat to our stability was the
approach of a convoy of two native-filled canoes proceeding
in the opposite direction. As they drew near, our crew stood .
up excitedly, waved their paddles, and began to jabber away
at the other natives in incomprehensible but apparently en-
dearing terms. This emotional outburst affected me perhaps

more than it did the approaching natives. Whereas they merely jabbered and waved in return, I was compelled to weave from side to side like a bobsled pilot to keep us all from capsizing.

It was a long, slow trip. Japanese destroyers were rumored to be in the vicinity, and we prudently hugged the coastline, feeling that it would be rash to venture into more open waters with an armament of one pistol and one rifle. There was always the danger, too, of a few inquisitive Zeros gliding down and using us for a little close-range target practice. Eventually we reached the native village we were heading for and plowed through the surf up to the beach, where the lieutenant, now awake, and I unloaded our cargo and dismissed our canoe as you might take leave of a taxi driver.

The natives who were helping our troops were all men serving either as sailors or porters. Many of them had moved up the trails with us a long way from their palm-shaded villages and their families. At each stop, however, we met and employed as bearers other native men who were in residence with their families, and these groups made an interesting spectacle as they would walk down a path. The men went first, unburdened and flamboyantly sensible of their superiority to the women. The women followed along silently under the weight of big sacks of bananas, mangoes, coconuts, and babies, mixed more or less at random. Along with a fairly domesticated pig or two, the fat-bellied children brought up the rear of the procession, skipping along among the trees that flank the path, nibbling at a piece of fruit picked off Mother's back, and sometimes, during long halts, sailing toy boats in tropical creeks just as if they had been in Central Park.

It was essentially a male's world, and on an important occasion, like the natives' payday, the women would withdraw discreetly to the side lines. The men who had been working for us would assemble in single file and parade expectantly to a grass hut, in front of which they would stand in line to receive the provisions with which they were partly rewarded for their efforts in the Allies' behalf. At one such ceremony I attended, most of the natives wore their customary garb of a rather dirty loincloth, but there were a few splendid sartorial exceptions. Four of them, responsible boys who were allowed to pack rifles, were clad in navy-blue shirts and skirts, and one, a handsome figure who was clearly a leader among men, stalked out of the hut in dazzling white underclothes, the envy of every native within sight. He was the paymaster, I later learned. As the lesser natives trudged by him, he handed each one a can of meat and two long sticks of the harsh trading tobacco on which they somehow thrived. I was impressed by the quiet and orderly nature of the performance, and commented on it to an Australian standing near by. "Yes," he said, "they're docile and friendly now." He paused slightly, then added, "A year ago they'd have eaten you."

We lived, from time to time, in villages deserted by the natives because of the war but retaining such embellishments as the huge and beautiful butterflies, high-voltage fireflies, whirring yellow-necked pheasants, noisy white parakeets, and the myriad insects that inhabit the region. A new feature of many of the native villages in New Guinea was the foxhole, something we soldiers contributed in large numbers as a precaution against enemy planes. We found our foxholes extremely useful on more than one occasion and sometimes ducked into them even when we didn't actually have to, since it is difficult in jungle territory, where the trees obscure your view of the planes you hear, to tell whose aircraft are cruising overhead. One of the commonest questions, even when the visiting planes were visible to all of us, was "Are they ours?" Pending a positive answer, the best policy, whenever the sound of motors got ominously loud, was to clamber into a hole. The day I heard somebody yell "Zeros!"—a warning we all respected—and automatically jumped into a trench which happened to be filled to knee depth with water, I was almost disappointed, on peeking up from my damp shelter, to see that the planes were ours. Being wet up to the knees, however, was nothing to complain about in that unpleasantly moist part of the world. It was not considered unusual to be wet up to the waist a good deal of the time, and the only object a soldier could have carried in one of his pants pockets with any real satisfaction would have been a sponge.

The fact that many of the native villages had been abandoned really worked to our advantage, since we were able to use their huts. These were, as a person might expect, one-room dwellings on stilts, covered by leafy roofs and equipped with floors conspicuous for their incompleteness. The flooring was of split bamboo, and there were usually substantial gaps in the surface. For some time I lived, surrounded by stilts, underneath one of these houses, while some of my pals lived upstairs. I attached my mosquito netting to the underside of the floor and placed my bedding on the ground, and whenever one of the fortunate individuals billeted upstairs walked around, a shower of dust sifted down on me, much of it into my eyes. I began to think bitterly that if the local architects had only been more conscientious about their work I might have slumbered more comfortably and cleanly. Then I was told that the natives deliberately left gaps between the floorboards for the sake of their pigs and other livestock, which dwelt beneath them and subsisted on whatever happened to drop through the cracks when the family was dining. At the time I welcomed this fascinating information, but I wasn't sure later that I wouldn't have felt better if I hadn't known I had lived like a pig.

13

On Land, on Sea, and in the Air

THE ROLE of the infantryman in warfare is conventionally supposed to be more or less analogous to that of the tortoise in his celebrated race. While aviators, sailors, tank men, and other members of the armed forces gambol about us like so many hares, we infantrymen sluggishly plod on foot toward the finish line, arriving there, of course, in time to do the major share of the dirty work. The Americans who did most of the dirty work, including the fighting, in the New Guinea campaign were the infantry. We were the plain, old-fashioned, pedal kind of infantry, but from time to time we found ourselves playing the more specialized parts of air-borne infantry. These extracurricular activities were a complete surprise to us, as so many things in combat are. We never had any training in the technique of air-borne infantry, but boy, were we air-borne!

Many of us, after flying from Australia to New Guinea, were also ferried by air over the Owen Stanleys. One group, however, made the trip on foot, matching the dizziest accomplishments of any alpine troops. They had to cut their way through jungle all the way across. It took them precisely forty-two tortuous days, whereas it took the rest of us just forty-two minutes to fly the same distance. Among other things, during their six-week jaunt, they were generally soaking wet, rarely had enough to eat, got malaria, ran into Japanese patrols, and, at certain uneasy moments, had to step gingerly along narrow ridges only a couple of feet wide and flanked on either side by apparently bottomless precipices. Our flights toward the front were our first association with planes. Later we had others. The members of the regimental band we had with us, for example, were mustered, not long after they had been flown to Papua, into an improvised aerial-supply detachment. Leaving their instruments behind them on the ground, they made daily flights over the jungle, dropping food, ammunition, and other equipment—by parachute or in padded bundles—to the rifle companies pushing up the trails. It was hazardous work. The transports were unarmed, except for whatever weapons the individual men on board happened to have with them, and in addition to the danger they would obviously have faced if any Zeros had intercepted them, they ran the risk, while flying low over hilly terrain, of bumping into the countryside. A regimental commander, who wanted personally to inspect the results of a dropping mission, was killed along with seven other soldiers when the plane they were on went down in a remote part of the jungle. They were buried there; it would have taken four days to carry their bodies back to Port Moresby.

Riding across the mountains on a transport was so short and simple a trip that it was hard to realize, when nothing untoward occurred, that there could ever be anything to fret about. On one such flight, however, several other passengers and I spent a few nervous minutes contemplating our fate when we gathered from the actions of a crew member staring anxiously out of a window that some Japanese fighters were heading our way. It turned out that he was looking at another transport, similar to ours, burning on the ground. We didn't know what had occasioned this accident, but we were all somewhat relieved at the sight of the blazing ship, perhaps because we felt that if we had departed a few minutes earlier the plane in the forest might well have been ours.

We were helped by planes in obtaining observation for our artillery fire. Slow-moving, nearly defenseless Australian Wirraways hovered boldly above Japanese positions, watching our shells burst among them and insolently inviting the enemy's antiaircraft to fire upon them and thus disclose hidden positions. When one of these cumbersome planes somehow managed to shoot down a Zero that had attacked it, the deed was regarded as miraculous and the Army newspapers featured deservedly breathless accounts of this singular example of airman biting dog.

Although we were fundamentally ground soldiers, we spent a good deal of time, too, on the water. The quartermaster troops in our outfits, who had been trained largely in terms of railheads and road nets, had the dampest time of it, and for a while they found themselves conducting minor naval operations almost every night. Trawlers loaded with supplies for our advance elements would sneak up the northeastern coast of New Guinea under cover of darkness and anchor several hundred yards off shore. It would then devolve upon the quartermasters to unload the cargoes and to do it quickly. Stark naked, with waves pounding over their heads, they pushed rowboats and native canoes out through the breakers, transferred heavy cases to them from the trawlers, and propelled them back to the beach, making dozens of exhausting trips without rest in order to get the vulnerable trawlers on their way again before daylight. Now and then the Japs would come over, shortly before dusk, and attempt to strafe the supply dumps hidden under trees just off the edge of the beach. Most of the soldiers around would prudently run for foxholes. One quartermaster lieutenant, however, whose prowess at coaxing supplies through the surf would probably have been respected even by the Coast Guard, would grab a tommy gun, rush out on the beach, and, as if he were the mother of some helpless brood, yell angrily at the Zeros trying to harm his nest of boxes and dare them to come down and fight within the limited range of his weapon. He never did hit a plane, but then the planes never hit him or his supplies, either.

Another quartermaster officer devoted himself with such zeal to establishing forward supply bases for advancing infantrymen that, during the early stages of the campaign, the small ships on which he ranged up and down the coast were not infrequently well ahead of our combat troops. He was given the apt nickname of "Commando," but he had little chance to enjoy it, since early one evening twenty Zeros caught a ship he was on, and three others near it, and set them all on fire with incendiary bullets. He must have been killed instantly; most of the other men involved, including a couple of generals, managed to swim ashore, a mile or so away, but no trace of him was ever found.

We had plenty of adventures in the air and on the sea, but on the whole, like most infantrymen, we stuck pretty close to the ground, sometimes on rainy days being stuck in it up to our waists. On the north side of the mountains, we moved from place to place, with rare exceptions, on foot. Even on the south side, there was no great abundance of vehicles, once you got away from the Moresby area. American engineers had constructed peep trails here and there; riding on them, however, was not a joy. One day I took a trip in a peep up a mountain trail that was, naturally, twisting. The road was barely wide enough for the car, and we had to duck at intervals to avoid low-hanging vines that were seemingly determined to clout us in the face. A peep, despite its smallness, is a powerful machine, but I saw one of them abruptly halted by a single jungle vine. Its driver noticed that the vine, swinging down across the trail, had looped around his front bumper. On the theory that a peep can do *anything*, he stepped hard on the gas. His front wheels were promptly lifted off the ground. We had to travel most of the way in the lowest of gears. The fastest recorded time for the distance we covered, eleven miles, was one hour and ten minutes. We made it in two hours, which wasn't bad, considering that a bridge broke down while we were on top of it. It was repaired by some roving engineers, assisted by a fat-bellied native boy who waddled out of the woods bearing on one shoulder a log three times his size. We went up and down hills so steep that a

motorcycle stunt rider would probably have declined to tackle
them even if promised immortalization in the newsreels, and
every now and then our wheels would, in a teasing fashion,
skid along an inch or so from the edge of the road, which was
also the edge of a distressingly perpendicular cliff. The driver
of the peep, a horseman by profession, complained bitterly
that he would never again get a kick out of participating in a
mere rodeo, and I had the novel experience of returning from
an automobile ride with a blister on my hand from hanging on.

Even such rollicking journeys as that were out of the question on the north side of the Owen Stanleys, where the few
usable peep trails were employed solely for the transport of
matériel and slightly wounded casualties. (Men with serious injuries were brought back to field hospitals by litter, on
the shoulders of native bearers; driving over the bumpy trails
would have been too rough for them.) The only extensive ride
I had the whole time I was over the hill was at the end of a
grueling jungle march, when, though uninjured in any strict
medical sense, I certainly felt slightly wounded all over. Ten
other soldiers and I, all fully equipped and mighty tired,
spied a peep which contained only the driver and was heading toward our bivouac area a mile or so away. I do not know
if the peep, whose dimensions, after all, are puny, will ever
equal in carrying capacity the forty-and-eight box cars reputedly so popular in the last war, but I do know that
the eleven of us, with our packs and rifles and aches, leaped
upon the little car, practically obscuring it from view, and
went bouncing off happily toward camp, reveling in the sensation of not having to supply our own locomotive power.

14

Busy in Papua

A SOLDIER's estimate of the number of things he can accomplish during a calendar day rises amazingly as his service progresses. Selectees fresh from the dawdling civilian world are usually downright appalled by the Army's assumption that they can keep going at a prodigious number of physically taxing activities from before dawn to dusk; older hands are merely irked by schedules as crowded—and including tasks as unsavory—as the Black Hole of Calcutta; and even soldiers in combat, who don't have to bother about schedules because their day never ends anyway, are sometimes startled, in the few brief moments allowed them for reflection, by their own durability. As a selectee, an older hand, and finally a member of an American task force in New Guinea, I was in turn appalled, irked, and startled.

At ten o'clock one evening, at our camp in a tiny native village on the coast north of the Owen Stanleys, I was notified that I was about to participate in a little expedition which, as it turned out, kept me rather fully occupied for nearly twenty-four hours. I was just going to bed when the news came. I hadn't had much sleep the night before because a lot

of planes had been flying around overhead and I had put in
what I judged to be a fairly creditable day's work since. When
I was told that I was to be permitted to go up to the front on
a tour of inspection along with an officer and one other soldier, I abandoned all notions of sleep and spent the next two
hours getting ready, which consisted mainly in taking an in-
ventory of what possessions I would leave behind. Anybody
planning a trip in the New Guinea combat zone selected his
impedimenta with great care and with a negative approach,
knowing that whatever he decided to take along would undoubtedly have to be carried for the greater part, if not all,
of the journey on his own back. After a good deal of delibera-
tion I gambled that we'd return by the next night and accordingly ruled out everything except a rifle, a bandoleer of
ammunition, and a filled canteen.

The officer, the other soldier, and I were able to save considerable walking, which was ordinarily the only way of getting about in that area, by making part of the trip forward
on a small trawler that was moving up the coast under cover
of darkness, carrying ammunition to the front-line troops.
Shortly before midnight a dim shape appeared offshore and
the three of us were rowed out to it. We swung up over the
rail and onto a deck piled high with cases of ammunition,
where we made ourselves as comfortable as one can be on top
of boxes of grenades. The master of our trawler, a drab vessel
some forty feet long, was a scrawny Australian wearing only
a pair of shorts and a sleeveless sweater several sizes too big
for him. His assistant was a fat fellow with what I took to be
an Italian accent; he was dressed merely in pants. The rest

of the crew consisted of a handful of Filipinos, every one of them a triumph of sartorial inelegance.

It was almost one o'clock when the captain gave the order to get under way, and we started chugging along at six or seven knots. We couldn't smoke because of the possibility that a glowing cigarette would be spotted by some enemy plane cruising hopefully above. We had all watched plenty of Zeros in action and knew what one or two of them could do to a trawler which was able to defend itself only with a couple of machine guns on antiaircraft mounts. Also, if we were attacked, we would probably have been exposed, surrounded as we were by ammunition, to a display of fireworks much more dangerously impressive than the gaudiest nightmares of a National Safety Committee spokesman. A full tropical moon was shining down on us, and under it we felt somewhat conspicuous.

We cruised along uneventfully until about two-thirty, when we suddenly came to a quiet, firm halt. The captain announced that we had run aground on a sand bar, a common hazard in those parts, and added gloomily that in his professional opinion we were badly stuck. We were still quite a few miles from our destination. Knowing that a trawler, however stationary, would naturally arouse the curiosity and attract the fire of any roaming Zeros as soon as daylight broke, we asked him if there was any chance of getting the ship off before dawn. After a consultation with his fleshy assistant, who was equally depressed, he told us that it might be done if we shifted a few tons of ammunition from the stern toward the bow. We devoted the next half-hour to hauling heavy cases forward. The boat still wouldn't budge. Then the captain sent a dinghy to drop anchor about thirty feet off to one side, ran a rope from it to a winch on the trawler, and tried to make the trawler pull itself off by its own power. We didn't move a nautical inch.

Hoping at least to get the cargo off by dawn, we Americans decided that we would proceed to our goal by whatever means possible and send back an unloading party. None of us had ever been in the neighborhood before, so we had no idea of where to look for the trail through the jungle that fringed the coast. The captain said that our best bet would be to row to the mouth of a certain river that cut the trail in two, proceed up the river until we came to the trail, and then take it. He said the river mouth was about a mile ahead. We finally prevailed upon him to pilot us and he got into the dinghy with us. By this time clouds had obscured the moon and we couldn't see much except a desolate shoreline. Our confidence in the captain as a guide would probably have been less wholehearted than it was had we known, as we found out the next day, that the river mouth he had mentioned was actually within fifty yards of where we struck the bar. We rowed along steadily, taking turns at the oars and keeping a watchful eye on the shore for signs of life.

It had been rumored in the afternoon that the Japs might attempt a landing somewhere along the coast that night, and we knew that whatever of our troops were on guard at the water's edge would be highly suspicious of our craft and might easily mistake us for an enemy patrol. After we had rowed along for about an hour and a half without finding the river mouth, it became obvious that the captain was getting nervous. He pointed to floating logs and whispered hoarsely that they were boats, and he took every dark object on the beach for a soldier with his finger on a trigger. He finally stated his conviction that we had passed not only the river mouth but also the town we were heading for and the American lines, and were about to bear down embarrassingly on a village serving at the moment, we all knew, as a Japanese base. Fairly certain that we hadn't gone by any of the distinctive clumps of coconut palms that indicated a village on the seacoast, the three of us military men outvoted the captain and decided to continue. A half-hour later, a telltale group of trees loomed up.

As we drew in to shore, our officer told me to call for a guard, despite the captain's anguished protest that the response might be *Banzai* or some other unaffectionate cry. I yelled out. A few seconds later a figure emerged from the shadows on the beach and stood at the water's edge, pointing a rifle at us and demanding, in English, the password. We hadn't any idea what the current one was but gave him an old one in which the letter "l" appeared several times. The sentry was satisfied to the extent of agreeing to take us to the officer we had been told to report to. We left the Australian captain on the beach with his dinghy, after promising to send back a detail of men to unload his cargo, and finally reached the command post we were looking for shortly after five o'clock. At five-thirty, after arranging for the ammunition-unloading detail, we readily accepted the suggestion of an officer there that we take a nap. Somebody lent me a blanket and I spread it out on one of the few patches of ground in the dense jungle large enough to accommodate it. I took a head net out of my helmet, pulled it over my head, and dropped down on the blanket. There were a couple of knobby roots underneath it, but I scarcely felt them. I probably fell asleep in mid-air.

A little over an hour later the three of us were awakened. We had breakfast in a crude kitchen where a cook prepared pancakes and coffee in old biscuit tins over an open fire. Shortly after seven we set out up the trail toward the front, about three miles away. We walked past several ammunition dumps, camouflaged artillery positions, first-aid stations making ready to handle the day's inevitable traffic, and numerous muddy foxholes and trenches containing soldiers who had slept in them the night before and were preparing for a morning attack. They were wearing the same clothes we were—twill jackets and pants dyed a mottled green and dirtied by weeks of living in the mud—and many of them had greenish paint smeared on their faces and hands. One rifleman, as we approached, proudly pulled up the bottoms of his trousers and showed us that he had paint daubed all over his legs, too, evidently so that he could remain obscure even if his pants were shot off. On the way up we also passed a couple of well-trodden spots in the jungle where, we were told, the Japs had had machine-gun emplacements before the American advance had begun. We asked if any enemy prisoners had been taken there. None had.

We eventually reached our destination, which was the most forward command post. It consisted simply of a field telephone in a foxhole and a couple of empty ration cases to sit on whenever it wasn't necessary to duck. In jungle fighting it isn't possible to see much, even a short distance away, but you can hear plenty. When the morning's attack began, there was first the sound of our own planes skimming the treetops on their way to strafe the enemy positions. Now and then we would catch a glimpse of them tearing by overhead. After the planes came an artillery barrage, launched by the guns we had passed. We could hear the shells bursting up ahead of us. At the same time, from dozens of foxholes scattered throughout the jungle—in front of us, behind us, and on both sides of us—light and heavy mortars opened up. Then came the command for the infantry to drive forward, and the ping of our rifle bullets and the stutter of our machine guns began to blend with the noise of the heavier weapons. The Jap machine guns answered them, and the Jap mortars, searching for our own mortar positions, started to drop shells in around us. We could hear the shells coming long enough in advance to take shelter in trenches or down among the roots of the huge mangrove trees. Mangroves, which, like most jungle flora, are afflicted with elephantiasis, grow horizontally as well as up. Sometimes six enormous branches, all pointing in different directions and each as large as a giant oak, will sprout from a single mammoth trunk. Whenever a heavy mortar shell landed near by, even the mangroves seemed to quiver as the concussion rippled along the floor of the fantastically lush battlefield.

After a while the medical collecting troops, with Red Cross brassards on their arms, began to come slowly back along the trail, carrying and escorting wounded men toward the first-

aid stations. There was a constant flow of men along the
narrow track. In addition to the casualties, sweating officers
covered with dirt and frequently bleeding from minor
wounds would return to report on the progress their troops
were making. At the same time a stream of soldiers kept
moving up, some of them to carry on the attack, others to
deliver ammunition. We stayed at the command post for a
couple of hours, and then our officer decided to begin the
return trip. It was about eleven o'clock and the attack was
still on. We had a fourteen-mile walk ahead of us back to
the camp we had left the night before, and much of it was
over soft sand, over which we knew we couldn't make very
rapid progress. We walked back to where we'd slept earlier
in the morning, had lunch, and then started out on the last
eleven miles of trail, a stretch, coincidentally, involving the
crossing of eleven streams.

A mile or so out, we picked up an itinerant sergeant from
Brooklyn who had been waiting on the trail for someone to
come along and keep him company. We noticed with surprise
that he wasn't armed, and he explained that he was assigned
to a noncombatant unit called Graves Registration, which
has the responsibility of burying men killed in action and
making detailed records of the circumstances. He had run
out of official forms, he told us, and was heading toward the
rear to replenish his supply before, he added with deep concern, his work piled up on him. For the rest of the way he
regaled us with anecdotes about his wartime specialty, for
which he had prepped, he told us, at a place in which the
opportunities for useful experience were unparalleled—the

morgue at Bellevue. As we listened to him, we realized that
at last we had found the perfect example of a selectee placed
by the Army's classification experts in the most suitable martial niche.

For more than half the way the trail followed the beach.
We plodded along with the sun beating down on us and our
feet sinking into the sand at every step, soon reaching the
river near which we had been forced to disembark from the
trawler the night before. That was when we learned how far
our geography had been wrong when we began our cruise
in the dinghy. The trawler, presumably unloaded, was still
there, held firmly on the sand bar. We crossed the stream by
means of a bridge some of our engineers were just finishing
up. We had moved on a mile or so farther down the coast
when we heard planes overhead. They were Japs. They flew
low past us, the red balls on the underpart of their silver wings
disturbingly large and clear, and we could hear the rattle of
their machine guns and a few moments later the dull explo-
sions of bombs. We were protected from aerial detection at
that point by mangroves, so we climbed out on some of their
horizontal limbs to try to get a better view of the proceedings.
A number of our fighter planes came down out of the sky, and
we saw the start of a couple of dogfights. Then all the planes
disappeared into the clouds. Later we heard that the trawler
and the bridge had both been damaged.

Although the destruction of a bridge was of course a decided inconvenience, it was not necessarily a calamity. The
natives, who as a rule wore nothing but loincloths and sometimes seemed rather to enjoy getting wet, didn't bother with

bridges at all unless the water they wanted to cross was over their heads. Then they would build a bridge by simply throwing a single log across the stream. Americans are more used to bridges, but we learned to get along without them. Of the eleven rivers we had to cross, only four were bridged at all, three by logs so slim and slippery that after contriving to get across them we felt as smug as tightrope-walkers. The seven other rivers we forded. At first we carefully removed our shoes and stockings each time and, when it seemed advisable, stripped from the waist down. As we grew more and more tired in the late afternoon, we took to not bothering with this, a neglect which we always regretted when we got to the other side and had to hike on with water sloshing around inside our shoes. Near the end of the trip we came to a stream which at its shallowest fording point had a maximum depth of about five and a half feet, near the far side of the crossing. On this occasion we stopped, removed all our clothing and equipment, and piled it on our heads. I rolled my stuff into a compact bundle, balanced it on my helmet, and put my rifle on top of everything else. I got along all right until I hit the deep spot. Then my helmet came down over my eyes, the water came up over my nose, a nasty current grabbed at my legs, and I felt that my rifle was slipping off, a feeling which turned out, a second later, to be regrettably accurate. When I finally retrieved the rifle from the river bed, after considerable underwater groping, it was a pathetic-looking weapon, full of sand and the promise of untold rust. As I carried it forlornly toward camp, which we finally reached at seven-thirty in the evening, I realized that the necessity for cleaning it as soon as possible had dispelled whatever lingering uncertainty I had had about my activities upon arrival. I knew then that I wouldn't be frittering the whole night away sleeping.

15

Our Fuzzy Friends

ONE of the permanent effects of this war, no matter what happens at the peace tables, will be a decline in movies with South Sea island settings. American soldiers who have returned from the Southwest Pacific will be unable to refrain from laughing out loud at the alluring women and romantic scenery exposed to their knowing, skeptical gaze, and Hollywood will have to change its line. If Dorothy Lamour and her luscious colleagues want to get out before it's too late, I'd suggest that they toss aside their wrap-arounds and dress themselves in Central European finery. This would assure them of a chance, for a while at least, to impersonate, imaginatively, seductively, and no doubt profitably, the belles of one of the few areas American soldiers have not yet thoroughly explored. Nobody in the movies or anywhere else is going to get very far trying to convince Americans who have been in New Guinea, for instance, that it is a garden spot or that its ladies are lovely, passionate flowers. I saw a lot of them and saw a lot of American soldiers near them, but I never saw any soldier so much as hold hands with one of them. Some of us, admittedly, stared with interest at their eccentric shapes, but it was always in a purely academic way. For the men of Papua, the women there may have a certain charm, but to us transients they were an unseemly bunch. I'm sure that they would say, and have said, the same of us.

Leaving the gross subject of sex aside, I'd say that the better we American soldiers came to know the permanent residents of this island, the more we appreciated them. At times they were our sole supply lines, as valuable as a railroad and somewhat surer. A railroad can always be blown up. When Japanese planes came toward a procession of native carriers, however, they merely dived into the jungle. Sometimes, to be sure, they remained there for two or three days, but almost invariably they came out again. Each group of natives working for us had a military organization of its own. The ranking member was a native police boy, often proudly wearing corporal's stripes, who carried an old-fashioned rifle. I never saw a police boy fire his weapon and had no idea whether or not it was loaded, but it commanded vast respect among his mates, who were unarmed and carried only a rolled-up fiber sleeping mat, a handful of tough vines, a long pole, and forty pounds of Allied impedimenta. Each group was also supervised by an Australian belonging to an organization called Angau—Australian New Guinea Administrative Union, I think the letters stood for—who tried to soothe his men when the Zeros approached, accompanied them up and down the difficult trails, and made sure that none of them was carrying more or less than his allotted load of forty pounds.

Before beginning a jungle march, we dumped into a pile

the extra equipment we couldn't carry ourselves, and the natives gathered around it like children examining gifts, while the Angau man, without the aid of scales, judiciously lifted each object and estimated its weight. Most of the natives, after receiving their assignments, worked in pairs, toting eighty pounds between them. They tied their load to a pole with their vines, put the pole on their shoulders, and then strode swiftly down the trail. They were incredibly fast. One day, when my company had to move thirteen miles, the natives started off just as we did. We were still about four miles from our destination, panting unashamedly, when we met the natives strolling back with their poles and rolled-up vines, heading for home as if they didn't have a care in the world. Covering twenty-five miles a day for ten days in a row apparently didn't strike them as anything noteworthy, but, in view of the fact that their wives act as porters when their own families move, I imagine they didn't find the work agreeable.

The majority of the natives we encountered were friendly and loyal to the Allied cause. By their standards of physical beauty we were certainly no more handsome than the Japs, but they were on our side. For one thing, they were well paid, and for another, they sensibly concluded, even without benefit of military commentators, that the white star of the Americans was the advisable one to get hitched to. Furthermore, they just didn't like the Japanese. When bringing one of our wounded back from the front lines, four of them would carry the litter gently and a fifth would walk alongside, holding a palm leaf over the injured man's face. They took no special pains when given the task of hauling back an enemy casualty. Some natives were employed by the Japs, who, at the time of their initial landing at Buna in the summer of 1942, coerced one whole local tribe into co-operating with them and in addition imported native carriers from New Britain. We captured half a dozen of those natives one afternoon, and when they were brought to our headquarters a couple of hours later, the natives who were there took delight in spitting on them.

The captive natives looked wilder than our own. They were liberally streaked with white paint, appeared cannibalistic, and would have fitted in perfectly with any casting director's preconceived notions of medicine men. Our carriers went in less heavily than they did for bodily adornment. Some of our men, though, were tattooed here and there, many of them wore flowers in their bushy hair (the women, however, did not), most of them dyed their teeth a sickly reddish brown with betel-nut juice, and a few, evidently dudes, treated their hair with this same clinging substance, causing it to turn an astonishing reddish-orange color. Their fuzzy hair was their most distinctive feature—Papua means bushy-haired in some language or other—and one Australian paper, in the course of raising a fund to provide them with Christmas presents in return for their favors to the Allies, referred to them in affectionate iambics as "The Fuzzy-wuzzy Angels of the Owen Stanley Range."

We scarcely considered the natives curiosities, probably because they were no odder than anything else in the vicinity. They were, besides, a comparatively subdued group, never pounding tom-toms, indulging in orgies, or dancing until all hours. Every now and then, to be sure, we heard shrill, frightening cries and assumed that one of them was beating his wife, but the practice didn't appear to be any more prevalent here than back home and was apparently condoned by the victims. Both men and women were notably modest. Although they wore practically no clothes, they nevertheless, for example, bathed as demurely as dowagers. I never saw a native older than eight or nine, in or out of the water, completely naked.

Comparatively few of the natives understood English, but it didn't much matter, since we rarely had an occasion to engage them in prolonged conversation. The Angau men were well versed in their gruff dialect and served as interpreters whenever we had any important messages to convey. Several of the police boys, moreover, were slightly better acquainted than their compatriots with our language and could usually pass the good word along. In emergencies, or quandaries, we could always fall back on sign language. I rarely heard anyone there talking to anyone else in pidgin English. There were a handful of natives who could even manage our irregular verbs, which they had learned to do from missionaries, but they were otherwise thoroughly un-Anglicized, or un-Americanized. For instance, they never used mosquito nettings, without which we wouldn't have dreamed of going anywhere unless we absolutely had to. The natives just let the mosquitoes bite them, and accordingly most of them were sprinkled with sores which had a tendency not to heal and which turned into itching, festering, tropical ulcers. Some of the natives,

too, were afflicted with a strange skin disease that covers their
bodies with grayish scales. We sedulously avoided those so
decorated. The natives, by the way, don't believe that by constant exposure to malarial mosquitoes they will acquire immunity; they just don't care. This attitude was shared by one
Australian I knew who had lived in New Guinea for twenty
years as the overseer of a rubber plantation. He once told me
that he never bothered with a netting and never took quinine
as a preventive against malaria. I asked him if he didn't get
sick. "Certainly," he said. "How often?" I asked. "Oh, every
three weeks or so," he replied.

That the natives and the Americans basically had little in
common is perhaps best proved by the fact that the former
regarded bully beef as a treat and gobbled up the stuff as
eagerly as we would have gone for breast of guinea hen. They
had other bizarre tastes; after one American rifleman had shot
a crocodile, the body didn't come to the surface for three days,
and then some natives leaped upon the mellowing corpse,
cooked it, and urged the Yanks to join the feast. The invita-
tion was declined with polite shudders. However, they
seemed, especially on the more sophisticated side of the
mountains, less concerned than one might expect with white
man's magic, showing practically no interest in our radios and
cameras. Unlike all natives of fiction, they were neither excited nor terrified when someone attempted to snap their
picture. They just took photography for granted. Also, instead
of standing around gaping when we turned on the radio,
they listened contemptuously a moment or two and then
walked away. The natives were no fools.

16

Housekeeping

AFTER a couple of months in the jungle an American soldier is apt to present so untidy an appearance that his own mother, if she recognized him at all, might be inclined to pretend not to. Many of the infantrymen in New Guinea, perhaps influenced by the unbridled, tropical growth that surrounded them, permitted their beards to flourish unrestrained. The shaggy faces, together with the worn, mud-soaked uniforms, gave them the formidable appearance of frontiersmen, which, I suppose, they were. Each member of my unit arrived in Papua with two new twill uniforms dyed a mottled green; the rest of our equipment was similarly camouflaged. An extensive wardrobe being unnecessary and burdensome on the north side of the Owen Stanley Mountains, most of us, shortly after crossing the range, were down to a single suit, which quickly got bedraggled. This we washed in a stream whenever we had a chance and then put it back on wet. We had no better way of drying clothes, and besides we wanted to enjoy the luxury of our relatively clean uniform as soon as possible.

In the jungle, keeping clothed and fed and housed were

matters that could never be taken for granted. Upon arriving at a new camp site, we couldn't lie down and rest until we had created something to rest on or perhaps under. The ground was always acceptable as a last resort, but the floor of the jungle is seldom dry and it harbors a vast menagerie of things that crawl and sting. Eating, for the most part, consisted of each soldier's downing, cold, his daily share of the canned hash or the bully beef and hard biscuits that comprised our regular diet, but when it was possible to prepare more elaborate meals, stoves were set up, water obtained and boiled, and many other odd jobs done by K.P.'s who would have been delighted if, as in the old days, they merely had had to wash several hundred dishes. Although most of us lost weight, the continuous heat and humidity, rather than any lack of supplies, were responsible for this. There was an ample quantity of food, if little variety. As a civilian, I often, by reason of economic necessity, worked at night in an environment that was not at all conducive to temperance, and often, by reason of choice, breakfasted the following, gray morning with my mother, who used to watch with silent alarm as my ill-treated stomach reacted with disdain to the conservative remedies I tried to press upon it. I sometimes wondered what she would have thought if she had been able one morning to watch me gorge myself on an exceptional treat whipped up by our mess sergeant, who, tired of serving the same old dishes for three meals every day, had ingeniously contrived to provide us with a breakfast of bully-beef fritters.

While eating and sleeping, and often while fighting, we soldiers in the jungle stayed reasonably close to the trail, as a precaution against getting lost in the matted growth on either side. The trail, or what we thought of more as The Trail, had as much significance in these parts as Main Street in any town back home. There was rarely more than one trail anywhere. Sometimes it was a fairly dry ridge between two neck-deep swamps; at all times it was the sole highway over which the men and matériel of battle could flow. In New Guinea we marched along many jungle trails as we shifted our headquarters from one site to another. We were always accompanied by native carriers, who marched at some distance ahead of us, striding effortlessly, our equipment tied by fiber ropes to the long carrying poles they rested on their seemingly tireless shoulders. When we traveled over unfamiliar trails, we could tell which way to go by observing the naked footprints of the carriers. On the northern coast of Papua the trail often emerges from the jungle and runs along the beach for a mile or two before cutting back into the jungle, and as we plowed through the soft sand, ordinarily our only means of judging when the trail left the seashore and re-entered the jungle would be to study the impressionable sands as thoughtfully as Robinson Crusoe ever did.

The native carrier bore, in addition to his normal load of forty pounds, only a few ounces of personal equipment. For an extended trip most natives took along a small sleeping mat of palm leaves, rolled up around a change of loincloth. Natives do not bother with such white man's accessories as canteens. Whenever they feel thirsty, they tie their ankles together with a vine, hunch themselves up the trunk of a palm, and knock down some coconuts. On occasion they would gladly dislodge an extra coconut for us in exchange for a single cigarette.

It is easy enough to work up a thirst in the tropics while you are just sitting down. While you are on the move, thirst is as faithful and unshakable a companion as a small, determined dog. One of the most delightful messages I have ever read was a note on fancy blue stationery propped on a forked stick in the middle of a trail, informing a party I was marching with that some husked coconuts had been cached two feet to our left. They had been placed there by an Australian who was leading a group of carriers along the trail half an hour ahead of us and who rightly figured that by the time we reached his communication we would earnestly appreciate his gift.

On another hike we walked for two miles through a field of kunai grass, which sometimes attains a height of six feet or more but affords no protection against the tropical sun. It beat down on our heads constantly and presently gave us all the annoying sensation that our skulls were being pounded by our helmets. At the end of that fiery stretch—when even a Regular Army colonel of twenty-odd years of service declared fervently that after the war he was going to be a soda-pop vender and sit where he could reach the ice without getting up—our joy at the unexpected sight of several coconut palms was inexpressible. When, further, a resourceful soldier produced some limes, the juice of which, mixed with fresh coconut milk, made our favorite tropical drink, we were almost as happy as if we'd seen snow.

Although we would have been perfectly content to camp

only in areas where coconuts were accessible, we frequently had to bivouac in less palatably vegetated spots. After marching all day, we sometimes stopped just before nightfall and hastily attempted to carve a home out of the undergrowth before darkness arrived. Once a group of us, trying to set up an officer's hammock after sundown, innocently attached one end of it to a tree somebody else had inconsiderately almost chopped down. A few minutes before the officer's bedtime, the mere pull of the hammock caused the tree, which was about a hundred feet high, to give way at its base. Luckily, it is practically impossible to fell a tree in the jungle, because its top branches inevitably become firmly entangled in those of a neighboring tree before it has fallen more than a couple of feet. Next morning we discovered that the tree we had blandly selected for the officer was also swarming with red ants. These insects are so ferocious that, upon finding you have been stung by one, your only consolation is that you were wrong in assuming that somebody had stabbed you with a hatpin.

Even by daylight we rarely saw much of the sky, because masses of foliage obscured our view overhead. Often we could hear planes flying above us and not see them, and we spent many uncomfortable moments waiting for someone—possibly a native, to whom the sight of a white star on a plane was as comforting as it was to us—to glimpse and identify the approaching ships. One afternoon, as some indisputably Japanese planes came toward us, I was occupied in digging a latrine trench. I had been proceeding in a rather leisurely fashion because of the heat and the nature of the task, but when I heard about the visitors I found myself shoveling with remarkable vigor. The planes circled around our vicinity, and every time they got past us I dug furiously and every time they came back again I dropped my shovel and sprawled down inside my handiwork. By the time they went away for good, I discovered to my surprise that I had completed an excavation of commendable depth.

Digging trenches was only one of a great number of things which we soldiers found ourselves obliged to do in the course of a campaign that must have been the war of survival the President was referring to. Beating the naturally antagonistic jungle was a difficult task. Merely lighting a fire, for instance, in an area that is consistently damp can become so irritating a problem that you will go to reckless lengths to solve it. An adventurous newsreel cameraman, desperately resolved to warm his canned rations, sacrificed a hundred feet of film one day to create an adequate blaze.

The handling of rations usually falls within the province of quartermaster troops, but in jungle warfare whatever work has to be done is done by whoever is there to do it. I spent a day in the unexpected capacity of an outdoors warehouse-man, supervising a bunch of natives who were stacking up hundreds of cases of provisions in a supply dump, and for the first and probably only time in my life I had complete charge of all the canned onions within a radius of a hundred miles. I also spent an entire night furtively operating a rowboat, ferrying supplies from shore to a vessel that was going to take them from our base to another one. Such activities and many others kept my days and nights fairly well occupied, but all in all my life in New Guinea was a cinch compared to that of the soldiers in the front lines, who, in order to kill Japs, had to incur endless risks and incredible hardships. Sometimes we soldiers who weren't in a position to destroy any of the enemy thought we were having it tough, but we weren't. After all—as one soldier in my outfit said reprovingly to another who, while scribbling a letter home, muttered that he couldn't bring himself to tell his family how awful it was—anybody involved in a jungle campaign who can find time to write about it is practically on a lark.

17

War Is Like This

EARLY in January, 1943, while the War Manpower Board was still fretting about who should or should not be drafted, Buna fell. A month or so later, the last of the Japanese ground forces who had been in Papua since the previous July were completely routed by American and Australian infantrymen. By the standards of large-scale warfare, it was a numerically unimpressive victory. On the Russian front, either side would probably regard as wasted any month that failed to produce more casualties than the total number of fighting men on both sides at Buna. War is not statistics, however. To the individual soldier, a minor patrol skirmish of no great strategical importance can, of course, rank with the greatest battles of history. The battle of Buna was not big, but it was hard and it was dirty. And long after the big Pacific battles to which it was the overture are finished, Americans who fought in the jungle and the tall kunai grass and the coconut groves of Papua will still be getting their mail in a hospital.

My part in the Buna campaign was a relatively inactive one. I didn't kill General MacArthur the Jap he had asked each of us to bag for him. I never even had the chance. My job was in a headquarters several miles behind the front-line positions, where I tossed around a lot of urgent and tactically significant message slips but no live ammunition. The areas I was in were generally so safe that my pals and I could still frivolously complain about mosquitoes when the boys up forward had long since ceased to show concern over any flying object less irritating than a machine-gun bullet.

A front-line soldier is rarely able to form any overall impressions of the action he is up to his neck in. In that respect I was lucky; I had a pretty good idea of what was going on before the fighting began and while it was under way. The Japs had marched across the Owen Stanleys and had withdrawn after getting to within some thirty miles of Moresby. Australian troops followed them back over the hills, and at the same time Americans, most of whom had been flown across the mountains east of the Japanese lines, closed in from the flank. It had been fairly certain all along that the Japs would make their last stand at Buna, their main Papuan base, in peacetime a rather dowdy coastal trading center and mission. Nobody knew exactly how strongly the Japs would be able to defend Buna. Aerial reconnaissance of the place was inconclusive; the skillful camouflage used by the Japs and the natural screen provided by the jungle effectively concealed their installations. It didn't take long to ascertain, though, that the enemy, expecting a siege, had constructed an elaborate series of fortifications, consisting mainly of earth bunkers reinforced with heavy logs that could withstand a direct hit from practically anything except a bomb. In the bunkers were slits through which machine guns could cover all likely approaches. Some of these bunkers held out until Australian infantrymen closed in on them behind medium tanks. Others were knocked out entirely by soldiers—Australian and American—who sidled up to them and tossed hand grenades through the vents, or managed to poke the nose of a tommy gun or automatic rifle inside and give the interior a thorough raking. Some Americans, to get up close to bunkers, slogged through neck-deep swamps, holding their weapons over their heads. When our troops finally entered some of the bunkers, with fixed bayonets and much caution, they found an unexpectedly large number of corpses, or thought they did. You can't ever be certain that a Jap who looks dead is. Judging by their ability to impersonate corpses, I'd say that the Japs have more than their share of dramatic talent.

Although Japanese exploits with knives have been well publicized, the New Guinea campaign, as far as I heard, did not disclose any great proficiency on their part in this line, beyond bayoneting bound victims, raiding hospitals and stabbing the patients, and committing hara-kiri, at all of which they had already been known to be adept. They bayoneted one ambushed American, unbound, half a dozen times without killing him. Out on a patrol, he was trapped by two of them. After felling him with one thrust, they bayoneted him five additional times and then sat down on what they presumed to be his remains and began to eat their lunch. The American, an incredibly durable soldier, regained consciousness an hour or so later and was startled to find two Japs on top of him, munching unconcernedly. Despite his wounds, he managed to remain motionless until they had swallowed

their last grain of rice and sauntered away. Then he gulped
down a handful of sulfa tablets, crawled back to his company, and reported in.

Many of our men fought for days without seeing anything
they could definitely identify as a Japanese. Enemy snipers
would conceal themselves so craftily in trees that, after the
branches had been riddled by machine-gun or automatic-
rifle fire, our soldiers still couldn't be sure whether or not
there had been anyone up there unless a body dropped down
or, if the sniper had tied himself to his post, dangled limply
from a branch. A good deal of the warfare was of a blind,
tentative nature, much of it fought from foxholes half filled
with water, in which grimy troops sometimes crouched for
several days. Sometimes the men had individual canned rations with them; sometimes a squad would get hold of a large
tin of bully beef and pass it around. One man would open it
up, eat his fill, put the lid back on, take careful aim, and fling
it into the next foxhole. This procedure would be repeated as
long as there were hungry men within range. This unortho-
dox and relatively simple method of feeding required so little
effort on the part of mess sergeants that occasionally, being
unable to perform their primary duties in their accustomed
manner, they would take it upon themselves to perform odd
little jobs. One day a mess sergeant and a cook, both dispirited
by their idleness, ventured up a trail, got in behind a Japanese
machine-gun emplacement, and tidied it up just as if it had
been a kitchen, except that they had no K.P.'s to help them.

The Japs were full of tricks, and some of our men fell for
them, once. One American unit, crawling through the jungle,

heard noises to their front, where they suspected the enemy was, and got ready to fight. "Hold your fire. We're the Aussies," a voice called out in a plausible accent. An American uttered a cordial and imprudent reply, and a moment later the Japs started shooting in the direction of his greeting. Many of the Japanese knew some English, and some who were not well-rounded linguists appeared to have been schooled in such phrases as "Give me a hand, Bud, I'm wounded," or "Got a cigarette?" Any American who heeded these pleas stood an excellent chance of being picked off.

In jungle warfare you never know what is going to happen next, and the tension that constantly prevailed in Papua affected not only the troops up front but those behind them, too. While my outfit was camping on the edge of the ocean, we continually imagined dangers lurking at sea. We knew, for instance, that the Japs had some submarines around, by which they had once or twice slipped in supplies at night. We wouldn't have been at all surprised if they had tried to use them to slip in reinforcements, and we frequently dwelt upon how embarrassing it might be for us if our little detachment found itself unexpectedly confronted with the task of resisting a battalion or so as it tried to make a midnight landing. From time to time mysterious flares would light up the night, dropped, presumably, by unknown planes that we could hear but not see. Other lights would flash out at sea, and we would debate soberly whether they were evidence of a naval engagement or merely heat lightning. Some men really got jumpy. One night, when I happened to be handling a field telephone, a frantic operator at an airfield a few

miles away shouted excitedly that the place was being
invaded and then lapsed into dismaying silence, leaving me
with the impression that he might well have been throt-
tled. Since that particular airfield not only was some distance away from where we had previously known the Japs
to be but also was a crucial supply base, his information was
alarming. Hurried orders were issued by our officers; companies were told to prepare to move out at top speed; wire
crews were dispatched to check the phones; warnings were
rushed to all units. Less than an hour later the report was
officially branded a false alarm started by a jittery sentinel,
and the incident was quickly forgotten as we all went back
to pondering such matters as who had won the naval engagement, unless, of course, it was heat lightning.

The next day there were some further taut moments when
a couple of soldiers ran into our headquarters with the astonishing revelation that they had been fired upon by a Japanese patrol far from where the enemy was supposed to be.
They had been walking down a trail some six miles away,
they said, carrying their shoes in their hands after fording a
stream, when they were attacked. Dropping their shoes, they
had wriggled along on their bellies to the stream, recrossed
it, and raced all the way back barefoot. We were perturbed
because two fairly high-ranking officers were somewhere on
that very trail, coming our way, and scarcely equipped to
withstand any determined assault. An hour and a half later
they turned up, traveling at a normal pace and wearing shoes.
It developed that they had fired a few highly misinterpreted
shots at some enticing coconuts on a palm tree. These in-

stances of temporary instability were, however, exceptions. On many more occasions soldiers in awkward spots displayed admirable coolness. One sergeant, who had been delayed while on a solitary mission in an unfamiliar stretch of jungle, was overtaken by darkness when he still had four miles to go. He was on a typical trail, full of twists, drops, mudholes, and protruding roots, and to navigate it at night without a flashlight would have been inconceivable. Faced with the unpleasant choice of spending the night where he was without a mosquito netting or floundering about and probably losing the trail altogether, he thought the situation over, then calmly groped around until he caught hold of a wire that was strung at the edge of the trail. He got home by feeling his way along the wire, having realized that a telephone line could be the shortest and safest distance between two points.

The men at the front in New Guinea were perhaps among the most wretched-looking soldiers ever to wear the American uniform. They were gaunt and thin, with deep black circles under their sunken eyes. They were covered with tropical sores and had straggly beards. They were clothed in tattered, stained jackets and pants. Few of them wore socks or underwear. Often the soles had been sucked off their shoes by the tenacious, stinking mud. Many of them fought for days with fevers and didn't know it. During one comparative lull, an inquisitive medical officer with a thermometer inspected some hundred men, and everybody involved was surprised to find that sixty of them were running temperatures of from two to three degrees above normal. Malaria, dengue fever, dysentery, and, in a few cases, typhus hit man after man. There was hardly a soldier, among the thousands who went into the jungle, who didn't come down with some kind of fever at least once. Officers and men were equally bedraggled. They ran similar fevers, ate the same dreary rations, and wore the same shredded garments, without any insignia of rank. Salutes were rarely exchanged, the use of military titles was discouraged, and, within the hearing of enemy snipers, whose favorite targets were those with authority, an officer would look downright hurt if any subordinate had the tactlessness to address him, in a carrying voice, as "Sir."

The fact that our troops were, on the whole, a somewhat slovenly-looking lot bothered no one except a few dashing staff officers fresh from the rear-area laundries, who came up forward on formal inspections or on sight-seeing trips. They were disturbed only as long as it took for them to achieve the same fraternal sloppiness, which was not long. Even our most dilapidated colonel, however, looked pretty sharp compared to the average Japanese. Most of the Japs we faced had had more jungle experience than any of us, but the fact that they could perhaps identify more tropical plants than we could had not rendered them less immune to the malaria-spreading Anopheles mosquito, which never makes friends, or to hunger, which was more manifest in their ranks than ours, despite the popular theory that a Japanese can exist practically forever on a penny's worth of rice and a handful of honorable fishheads.

The termination of the existence of a lot of Japanese around Buna was expedited by the ability of Americans to become tough to a degree that would undoubtedly have shocked any sensitive parents who saw them in action. There were numerous cases of soldiers who withstood incredible suffering in the common cause of killing as many of the enemy as possible and getting the damn war over with. There was the private first class who, painfully wounded in the groin one night, lay in a watery foxhole for thirteen hours with maggots crawling over him, stubbornly refusing to cry out for help because he knew that the slightest sound might give away his company's location. There was the private who, because of a shortage of medical orderlies, didn't bother to tell anybody when he was shot in the foot. He limped back to a field hospital carrying a bullet he had extracted from his legging, after it had gone through his shoe, not to mention his heel and ankle. He had walked to the hospital, several miles away, all by himself, and when a dazed doctor investigating this miracle asked if it hadn't hurt, he said no, not too much except when he stopped to rest. "So I kept going," he added. There was the lieutenant who for days lay, desperately wounded but conscious, within conversational range of his platoon, and who kept a diary until he died. Three men had tried to get to him, but when one was killed and the other two were wounded in the attempt, he asked a captain to forbid anyone else to come out and the captain reluctantly agreed because he couldn't spare the men.

The jungle was tough and the Japs were tougher, but the Yanks were the toughest of all. I stopped in at a hospital to talk to one of them, lying wounded on a bed far from the front, eating the first decent food he'd had for weeks, and able at last to get a bath and a cold drink whenever he wanted to. "Well, you're pretty lucky," I said, "to be out of all that. You'll have a fine rest now."

"The hell with the rest," said the soldier. "My brother was killed up there."

18

Purple Heart

When your best friend is wounded in action, you are supposed, according to all the scripts, to be right there and to take immediate avenging steps. When my best Army friend —a soldier named Dan Herr, who is very small and looks as if he would fall apart if you waved a rifle at him—was hit, I was ten miles away. I didn't even hear about it until a few hours afterward, and then only through a garbled field-radio message. A soldier in a combat zone cannot, of course, afford to become too excited about someone's having been killed or wounded. My buddies and I were reconciled, when we got to New Guinea, to the probability that some of us would never leave the place. My particular company was fairly lucky, as a matter of fact. Our combat duties did not require us to take an active part in the front-line fighting, and as a result most of us got by with skins unmarred by anything more deadly than a mosquito. There were exceptions. One of my friends looks all right now, but he has a little scar on his shoulder where there used to be a hole and a tiny piece of steel in the middle of what used to be a good lung. Another has been lying on his back on a hospital bed for so long

that lately the blisters on his shoulders have been bothering
him almost as much as his chest, down the length of which a
machine-gun bullet made a rather thorough tour. One man in
my company had the misfortune to catch malaria just before
the Japanese decided to bomb a hospital he was sent to, and
the bombing was fatally accurate.

This story about Dan Herr has a happy ending, but if anybody had asked me to bet when I first saw him after he was
shot that he'd be on his feet six weeks later—as he was—I
wouldn't have put up a nickel plugged as many times as he
was, which was five. We were both stationed at a native village along the north shore of the island, and early one afternoon he was picked to accompany some officers on a trip up
the coast aboard one of four small luggers loaded with ammunition and other supplies. They pulled out around three
o'clock and were supposed to reach their destination about
four hours later. Just before dark that evening, back at our
camp, we heard planes approaching from the east. We counted
eighteen. Never having seen more than three or four Japanese planes in the sky at once up to that time, we assumed
that these planes were ours, an opinion we hastily revised
when they got nearer and we saw that they were Zeros.
They didn't pay any attention to us. Maybe they didn't realize that the village below them had a lot of Americans hid-
ing around and under it, or maybe, sensing bigger game
ahead, they didn't care. At any rate, they flew straight on,
and we felt a lot better. Then we remembered the four little
boats, loaded with ammunition, out on the Pacific.

At that stage of the campaign the only means we had of

communicating with our forward elements was by radio. Every message had to be coded, and it seemed a long time that afternoon before we got a message off, asking if everything was all right. We couldn't help suspecting that if the Japs had spotted the luggers before they unloaded, everything probably wasn't. A while later we got our answer: "All four ships burning. Several dead." From then on, throughout the night, we received a string of messages. Many of them were garbled, but we gathered that the Zeros had dived down and strafed the luggers with incendiary bullets. One of the few messages that made sense was a terse one: "Herr and some others wounded." It is probably only during a battle, when you expect the worst, that you can experience a great sense of relief at hearing that a friend of yours has been wounded.

We didn't find out that night exactly who had been killed, how many had been wounded, or how badly hurt those who had been were. We didn't sleep much; everybody sat around in the dark speculating and hoping that things weren't as bad as our imaginations pictured. The next day we got our first real information from an old Australian seaman who had been on one of the boats, had swum ashore, and had walked down the trail from the scene of the attack. In a way, he was maddening. He had been there, all right, and had seen everything that went on, but, never having been introduced to any of the American soldiers and having no idea what any of them were named, he couldn't tell us with assurance which of our men were alive and which were dead. I mentioned Herr to him, but the name meant nothing. When I described

him as a small, skinny, blond-haired fellow, however, he remembered him well. "Ah, yes," said the seaman, using the
Australian equivalent of *mais oui,* "he got hurt the worst.
They machine-gunned him all over the place. I counted five
bullet wounds."

It was inconceivable to those of us who had been left behind that anyone of Herr's slight build could be shot that
often and survive, especially taking into consideration the
probable shortage of medical facilities up where he was. We
were sad and we were sore, because it seemed unfair of the
Japs to single out as a target a man so patently unable to absorb
that amount of punishment. We waited all day for more detailed radio bulletins to come in. We didn't get any—after
all, there was a war on and the welfare of a few casualties had
a low priority with our signal officers—but at least nobody
reported that Herr was dead, and I was grateful for that.

The next afternoon I was ordered to move up the coast myself, in a native canoe, to Oro Bay. Oro Bay is just a small
native village tucked under some coconut trees, indistin-
guishable from a dozen other native villages strung along
that thinly populated coastline. I had no idea whether or
not I would find Herr on my way up, but I knew that he
must be somewhere around there. Before I left camp, I spent
some time consulting the other soldiers in our company about
what I should take along for him, in case I did run into him.
We had most of his clothing and equipment, but we couldn't
see much point in delivering any of that to a man who had been
shot five times. Finally we decided that the most sensible
thing would be a carton of his favorite brand of cigarettes. We

didn't know whether or not he could smoke, but everybody agreed that I shouldn't go empty-handed. Even in the jungle, there were certain traditions about visiting patients in a hospital.

I reached Oro Bay just before dark and wandered back off the beach toward some tents I could see at the edge of the jungle. There were only a few of them, scattered around haphazardly; they constituted, I soon discovered, a field hospital. There are various stages of hospitalization through which a soldier wounded in combat passes. When he is hit, if he can't give himself first aid, he gets it from a medical-aid man, who crawls out under the enemy's fire, bandages him as well as he can under the circumstances, and drags him back to an aid station. (Now and then our medical-aid men got shot themselves.) After our casualties had been treated at an aid station, they would be moved to a portable hospital, where a doctor, who in better days would probably have howled at a nurse for giving him a sterilized gown bearing traces of tattletale gray, performed delicate operations stripped to the waist, ankle-deep in mud, in the beam of a flashlight. Behind the portable hospitals were the field hospitals, behind them the station hospitals, and finally there were the general hospitals, which really looked like hospitals. The establishment at Oro Bay was a field hospital and wasn't very impressive. Herr was there, all right. I found him in a tiny, one-man tent, with screened flaps, marked "Surgery." I could see him through the flaps, but I didn't go in. He was lying on his back on a cot, covered up to the neck with a bedsheet, and he looked dead.

I stood outside the tent for a few minutes, holding the carton of cigarettes and trying to detect some movement within. There wasn't any, so I went off to search for an attendant. I found a medical orderly in the next tent, and when I told him I wanted to talk to Herr, he said my chances weren't too good. "We just gave him a shot of morphine," he said, "and he'll be out cold for hours. And we're evacuating him by boat three hours from now." I asked if there was any likelihood of his waking up. The orderly told me that if he did become conscious at all it would be only because of the pain induced by his being moved. "He's pretty bad, you know," he said. "One bullet fractured his upper right arm, two of them got him in the left arm, and two more got him in each knee. We've got one of the bullets for him as a souvenir." I learned some time afterward that he had been brought there from a portable hospital. Before that, he had received first-aid on a beach, after a dinghy in which he was riding when the Zeros got him was finally rowed ashore. His first treatment had been the standard one given during the campaign. Somebody had come along with a package of sulfanilamide powder and poured it into his wounds. He was conscious the whole while, and at one point he asked a soldier to bring a general to see him. Herr had been carrying an envelope containing a few dollars up to the general. The soldier, not knowing exactly what was up, rushed to a tent where the general was taking a nap, woke him up, and gasped that a dying man had asked for him. The general jumped up, dressed hastily, ran to the beach, saw Herr, and began solemnly to say the final good-bys he assumed were expected of him. Herr interrupted. "Sir," he said, trying to roll into a respectful position and succeeding only in shedding considerable powder, "I'm sorry, but I guess I lost all your money." Herr was always a very conscientious soldier.

The medic told me I might as well go away and come back when they moved him. I hadn't eaten anything for some time, so I walked off to look for rations. I eventually found a soldier who had two cans of cold beans. He gave me one, which I ate. Then I went back to Surgery. It was getting dark, and I could barely make out Herr's head through the flaps, but I could see that he still wasn't stirring. The orderly came along and I asked him if Herr could smoke when he woke up. It seemed very important to me, for some reason or other, to get those cigarettes to him. The orderly said that Herr probably wouldn't feel up to smoking for a while but that he'd put the carton on the litter on which Herr was removed, so it would accompany him to the station hospital. "He was pretty lucky," the medic said. "He'll get a nice Purple Heart and a nice, long rest." I didn't feel especially envious.

A couple of hours later four soldiers came up to the tent with a litter to carry Herr down to the beach and load him on a rowboat that would ferry him out to a lugger which served as a hospital ship. They asked me to help them transfer him from his cot to the litter. I slipped my arms gingerly under some of the bandages that enveloped his limbs and the five of us lifted him up slowly. Herr started to moan and moved his head. That was reassuring. It was the first sign of life I'd seen in him. He opened his eyes, and when he saw me he let out a yelp and began talking quickly in a semi-delirious vein. Like most men who are wounded and carried away from their outfits, he hadn't any idea he would run into someone he knew for weeks, and he was startled. I figured that he thought he might be dreaming.

It was about a quarter of a mile down to the loading point, and I went along. All the way he remained conscious, talking in a faint voice and asking me to bend over so that he could hear me. Walking along a New Guinea trail is sometimes difficult when you are alone. It is considerably more difficult for four men carrying a stretcher and a fifth walking beside it. There wasn't any room on the trail for me, so I hopped along through the vines and roots alongside it, trying to stay next to Herr and lean over to talk to him. I asked him how he was feeling, and he said fine, which was obviously a lie, and I told him all the boys were rooting for him and were proud of him, and he asked me how they were, and I said fine. Then I told him about the cigarettes, which the medic had placed behind his head, and he thanked me politely and said they were just what he wanted, but I am not sure he knew what I was talking about. A lot of what we said didn't make much sense, probably, since he was a bit incoherent because of the pain and the morphine and I was mainly trying to keep my balance, stay close to the litter, and promise him that I wasn't going away. He knew I was, though, when they carried him out into the water and rested his litter on the seats of the rowboat. He asked me to ride along, and I said that I couldn't but that I would see him again soon, although actually, since he was going back from the fighting zone and I was going forward, it seemed doubtful then that I would see him for some time to come, if ever. Herr is extremely religious and I am not, and perhaps that's the reason I remember the last words he said to me, as we parted for what turned out to be only a month, more clearly than anything else which happened that day. "I know you don't believe in it much," he said, "but please pray for me." I did.

19

Australian Recess

THERE are many things a soldier misses in a combat zone, especially so austere a one as New Guinea, where, since the usual business transaction involved only the exchange of a cigarette for a coconut, we American troops threw away the coins in our pockets because we considered them excess weight. While not occupied with military duties, we used to reflect at length on the things we had left behind, and in every set of reminiscences the traditional wine, women, and song had a high priority. In the jungle we had little firsthand traffic with any of them. On one memorable occasion a friend of mine borrowed from an overstocked medical-supply depot a minute amount of alcohol, which, mixed with concentrated fruit juice and judiciously thinned with chlorinated water, made an acceptable and, it turned out, harmless potion. Aside from that, however, we were as temperate as institutional beer ads. We never concerned ourselves with women, except in the abstract, because the only ones around were natives, who were not, as I have observed before, Dorothy Lamour.

Of our trinity of interests, song came off best. For a while we had access to a short-wave radio, on which we received occasional tunes from home. Once we had moved to the northern, or business, side of the Owen Stanley Mountains, however, we had only our own voices. Among the things I will always remember about the Papuan campaign is the fact that I devoted a disproportionately large part of it to teaching a sergeant from Boston—who had done some night-club entertaining and went in for lighthearted numbers like *Tangerine*—the lyric of a rather dirgelike ditty fervently condemning lynching and calculated by its composers to depress all listeners. After diligent practice, he mastered the words, though he felt they would hardly help him professionally, but he never could get the tune, possibly on account of some vocal defect of mine. There was no reason for his learning the song or for my teaching it to him, but it gave us both something to do during the long hours when we might otherwise have merely been nervous. At that, the zeal with which he accomplished his mnemonic chore seemed to have no military ill effects. A few hours after he had memorized the last bitter couplet, he went out and won himself a Silver Star for gallantry in action.

It was much sooner than I could have hoped that I had a chance to hear some reasonably new songs, see a number of attractive women, and drink a small glass or two of wine. The opportunity came when I was suddenly sent back to Australia. Before sunrise one morning I found myself, along with other members of my outfit, boarding a southbound plane, and not long afterward I had lost sight of New Guinea. The sun came up while we were flying over the Coral Sea, and if

you think a tropical sunrise seen from ground level is one of
the most beautiful sights imaginable, you've never seen one
from the air. I had fallen asleep soon after we took off and was
awakened by another soldier's elbow. "Look," he said, and I
looked, and it was worth looking at. The sky was streaked
with giant gashes of purple and pink, and for the next half-
hour there was a varying display of violent splashes of color.
After the sky had quieted down, I dozed off again, and woke
up shortly before we landed at an Australian airport near a
certain city. Among the officials who came out there to ex-
amine our travel orders was a woman. I noticed that practically all the passengers, including myself, were staring at
her. We hadn't seen a woman of our own color for more than
two months. She was not at all pretty, but we couldn't help
gazing at her curiously for a couple of minutes. She didn't
seem offended. Working at that particular field, the first stop
on the route south, she was probably used to it. However,
when she started in on the job, she must have thought her
slip was showing.

I took three hot showers during my first twenty-four hours
back in Australia, but I still didn't feel clean; after you've
walked around in New Guinea mud for a while, you are apt
to think of yourself as permanently gray. Then, putting into
effect the program we had all planned for ourselves up north,
I invited a girl I had known before to have dinner and a few
drinks and hear some music. It was just as I'd pictured it.
It was, I guess, wonderful.

Australian girls, all in all, are neither as well dressed, nor
as good-looking, nor as elaborately educated as American

girls, but they have much to commend them, including an agreeable determination not to abet loneliness in American soldiers. Many of the girls we met were proud of their knowledge of Americana, and by way of demonstrating their international awareness they frequently quoted the words of a Broadway tune, learnedly discussed Hollywood, or asked us, in so many words, to buy them a coke. Australian women have been in uniform for so long now that no one regards a Waaaf (Women's Auxiliary Australian Air Force) or an Awas (Australian Women's Army Service) as an oddity, nor do the lady soldiers themselves exhibit any self-consciousness about being addressed as private, corporal, or signalwoman.

Practically all Australian young women are working, the majority of them in essential industries. One girl I got to know fairly well, who had begun working for an oil company at the age of sixteen and now, four years later, had a responsible job in its auditing department, worked two nights a week but still found time to volunteer for extracurricular wartime tasks. She had to work only a half day on Saturday, so she spent the afternoon visiting wounded soldiers at a hospital. She had all day off Sunday, so she was able to spend practically the whole of it at an American Red Cross Service Club, where, with dozens of other Australian girls, she ran a cafeteria that was one of the few eating places open on Sunday, a day on which many Allied soldiers could be found looking wistfully at the locked doors of stores, theaters, pubs, restaurants, and other establishments they wished were open. In what time she had left over, she made her own clothes. Australian wages are not high; despite her four years of service, and the fact that she had several other girls working under her, her pay, including the overtime for the two nights, came to two pounds ten shillings a week, or about eight dollars. She gave her family one pound of that for room and board, spent six shillings on carfare and lunches, and was thus left with approximately four dollars to splurge on everything else. She did not regard herself as oppressed or exploited, since she was earning the average salary for a girl of her age. She was saving money, she said, for a trip to the United States, a journey many Australians are eager to make. Considering what she has to save out of, whether she will attain her hope will probably depend less on her thrift than her durability.

A soldier returning to Australia may have, understandably, wanted a drink, but, like everyone else, he didn't have too easy a time getting one if he was at all fussy. In the city I happened to land in, the bars opened at eleven in the morning and closed, theoretically, at six, but they had usually run out of their daily quota of stocks considerably before then. Rye and bourbon had never been readily procurable, and Scotch was exceedingly scarce, unless you agreed with the Australians that the name Scotch could be applied, as they applied it, to a homespun distillation suitable only for the most tolerant of throats. Rum and gin were easier to buy, and lived up to their names. Beer, at eight pence halfpenny a glass —or pot, as they said—was usually obtainable, though it was becoming increasingly rare in bottles. An Australian's chances of purchasing any bottled liquor were slim, and during the limited hours when home-supply stores were open, long queues of civilians carrying the inevitable suitcases with which they shop would line up patiently on the streets, waiting doggedly but pessimistically, like theatergoers hoping that the S.R.O. sign over a box-office window will somehow be taken down. The resourcefulness Americans are supposed to show when exploring foreign lands generally enabled us to find *something* to drink. Once, when I was visiting some friends, we discovered to our dismay that there wasn't a potable around. Another American recalled having seen a case of dubious-looking bottles marked "Tonic" lying around in some shopwindow, and went off and got them. We opened one of the bottles, and, after discovering delightedly that it contained a dark and tasty beer, examined the lable more closely. From it we found out that what we were drinking—and how it got to Australia we never did learn—was a brew described by its manufacturers, now undoubtedly inactive, as being especially beneficial for nursing and convalescent mothers in the Philippines.

Although American soldiers down under drank less, if anything, than those in the States, having fewer opportunities, they were, at one peculiar time, accused of drunkenness on purely circumstantial evidence. The occasion was the return to Australia of some soldiers who had spent months fighting in the jungles and were brimming with latent malaria. The fusion of alcohol and malaria often produces a violent chemical reaction, with the result that the soldiers enjoying their first beer in a long time had the unhappy experience, a few minutes later, of collapsing. To them it indicated for the first time that they had the fever; to some onlookers who knew neither the men's medical nor martial histories, however, it indicated mass inebriation. Malaria hits you without warning, and if you've had a couple of drinks it is apt to hit you exceptionally fast. I remember waking up one morning, after a party, feeling terrible. I thought I had a hangover for an hour or so, but suddenly I felt very chilly and began shaking uncontrollably. Then I knew, of course, that what I needed to pick me up was not tomato juice but quinine.

On our return from New Guinea, we were received much more calmly by our Australian hosts than, as we had gathered from the press, soldiers back from combat zones were being received in the United States. Men who had been in action were no novelty down under, and a couple of months in Papua didn't, naturally enough, seem very impressive to a populace whose sons and husbands, if they had got home at all, usually had behind them a couple of years in the Middle East. Our Australian friends were glad to see us back, though, and we were glad to be there. Many of us, when we moved north, had no idea that we would ever be heading south again, having at the time a hazy notion that a more or less straight line would be the shortest and most likely route between two such points as Australia and Tokyo, but we were not disappointed at temporarily having to retrace our steps. A year before we never would have thought possible what, after all those months abroad, seemed perfectly logical to us: that on coming back from battle, we should get to a place as far from our own families as Australia and be greeted by its citizens with a cheerful "Welcome home."

20

Homeward

TEN years ago, or maybe even less, anyone who completed a successful crossing of the Pacific by air not only was regarded as lucky and foolhardy but stood a good chance of being acclaimed the performer of a prodigious feat. Today the members of the rather inclusive and informal society known as the Short Snorter Club—for membership in which anybody who has flown across any ocean, even a small one like the Atlantic, is eligible—are so numerous that the entrance of an initiate into their ranks is a matter of interest to nobody except, possibly, the initiate. I flew across the Pacific, from Australia to California, and it was a much less eventful flight than many I have made over drier and shorter courses. Once, while I was being jolted along from Cleveland to Chicago, an otherwise thoughtful hostess spilled a whole cardboard container of coffee on my best suit, a gabardine, and I arrived at my destination, according to an inelegant friend who met me, smelling like an unwashed cup. Nothing half so exciting as that occurred over the Pacific. Although we were in the air for more than forty hours in our series of hops, we never encountered weather rough enough to cause the other passengers and

myself to fasten our safety belts. It would be untrue to say
that we weren't aware of the possibility that we might find
ourselves in a position in which we would be pleased if a sea-
gull landed on our heads, but it is difficult to feel a sense of
impending doom when you are cruising steadily and smoothly
over mile after mile of seemingly placid water. Except for two
minor inconveniences, our trip could have been considered
comfortable by any standards. One was that the seats on
which we dozed all the way to Hawaii were removed there,
and we spent the last, long lap squirming unhappily on mail
sacks. The other was that we were forbidden to smoke inside the plane.

I hadn't expected to be ordered back from Australia as soon
as I was, and why I was is, as we soldiers like to say under
lay cross-examination, none of your business. I had supposed
that I would be stationed in the Southwest Pacific Area until at least the end of the war, and was therefore surprised and
elated at the thought of going home. While steaming out of
San Francisco on our way to the South Seas, and during the
many months we lived there, both in Australia and New
Guinea, the men in my company had frequently dwelt fondly
on the blissful day when we would sail back under the Golden
Gate Bridge or catch sight of some equally homey landmark.
It had taken us weeks to make the westward crossing. By air,
I knew, the trip would take only three or four days—two or
three calendar days, because of the international date line. I
hoped my family wouldn't receive too much of a shock when
I called them up from California and told them I was home,
or at any rate a mere three thousand land miles from home.

None of the passengers were allowed to send cablegrams be-
forehand hinting that they were on their way. We found
our departure hard to believe ourselves until a sergeant,
weighing our baggage in a dimly lighted hangar on the night
we left, matter-of-factly scribbled the name of our destination on a tag with the bored, casual manner of a man who
had been through the same routine many times before and
wished we would take off so he could go to bed.

There were eight passengers besides myself: a general and
two aides, with all of whom I had served in the Southwest
Pacific; an Army Air Forces navigator going home for a rest
after having been wounded on a bombing mission; a Navy
lieutenant from a torpedo-boat squadron; two civilian repre-
sentatives of a plane-manufacturing firm, who had been in
Australia observing their product in action and wildly ac-
cumulating souvenirs; and a war correspondent. As we waited
for the ground crew to get our huge, four-motored transport
ready, we were given a mimeographed set of regulations telling us how to behave while aboard and instructing us always
to wear our lifebelts in the air. We wandered over to a booth
where the ubiquitous American Red Cross was handing out
coffee and doughnuts, said good-by to some American friends
who, gallantly concealing their envy, had driven to the field
to see us off, and were roundly kissed farewell by a number
of Aussie girls serving as chauffeurs for American Army officers. Some of us were wearing winter uniforms and some
our summer ones. It developed that all of us were dressed
wrong. Those of us in light clothes shivered while we were
flying and those in heavy ones suffered whenever we came

down on a tropical island. We were in the air just a bit more than half the time we spent crossing the ocean, so our complaints about the heat and the cold were almost evenly divided.

It was a little after midnight when we climbed aboard, tied our orange-colored lifebelts around us, and settled back in our seats. I couldn't see the other passengers in the dark interior of the plane. Our chairs were the sort of reclining type you might find on any Stratoliner. The most nervous moment of the entire flight came right at the start when, as we soared off the ground, long streaks of blue flame burst from a couple of the motors. A member of the crew scuttled back from the nose of the ship and pressed his face against one of the windows, shining a flashlight on the guilty motors and looking, I thought, apprehensive. Presently, without saying a word, he went back, and a moment later the flames died down. We didn't learn until morning what had happened; then we heard that the pyrotechnical display had been merely the result of too rich a mixture of fuel and that everything had been under control all along.

We landed just after dawn at an Army airfield on New Caledonia, and while we were fumbling for cigarettes we got a good look at each other. The war correspondent had equipped himself for the ride with an armful of paper-backed novels, which he graciously offered to share with us. Before the trip was over, I had read one and a half detective stories and a rather cloudy romance entitled *Gypsy Lover*. The rest of us hadn't brought much reading matter, but I did have two roasted chickens, which a generous lady had cooked for me and packed into a bon-voyage hamper. The chickens provided us with several fine if slightly greasy snacks. As a matter of fact, we were well fed throughout the trip. There were sandwiches and coffee on the plane and more robust meals wherever we stopped. Our first breakfast, at an American Army mess on a dusty, red-clay, New Caledonia hill, consisted of fruit, bacon, hot cakes and sirup, milk, coffee, and one egg. The mess boy, a native, was apologetic when he informed us that there was a restriction on eggs, and told us, by way of making amends, that each of us could have his egg cooked according to his own taste. I said I'd have mine fried, sunny side up, and he nodded understandingly, as so many one-time strangers in the Pacific now do in response to American jargon.

While enjoying my egg, I met the crew of our plane. They were civilians, but, like most civilians who have anything to do with the Army in a theater of operations, they were in uniform. They had been flying all over the world during the past year and agreed that on the whole they preferred the African run. "That Cairo!" said a youthful navigator enthusiastically. "That's the place for me." He added that he didn't particularly mind flying across the Pacific but that it got dull riding over all that open water without even a Shepheard's Hotel at the other end. Our crew had flown in from the United States just nine hours before heading back and were due to be relieved by a fresh bunch at Hawaii. They were glad to be getting off there; they understood you could buy pretty good shoes in Honolulu, and without a ration card.

It was early in the morning when we took off again. The

motors once more belched blue flame, and we all nodded to each other knowingly. We reached our second stop, one of the Fiji Islands, in time for a late lunch at an American officers' club.

The camp we stayed in there was a far more imposing military reservation than the ones we had been used to in New Guinea and Australia, and it showed how firmly the United States Army has established itself in odd corners of the South Seas. The club at which we ate served after-dinner liqueurs, the plumbing was modern, the barracks were substantial and permanent, and the magazines and newspapers were considerably more up-to-date than any we had been reading farther to the west. When we were told that we would be sleeping there overnight and would take off at dawn, so as to be sure to hit our next goal, a tiny coral island, in daylight, we were not sorry. We lounged on the clubhouse porch for a couple of hours, chatting with pilots who had been fighting in the South Pacific. It was raining, so we didn't do any sightseeing. The weather cleared up during supper, and afterward I wandered down a dirt road and dropped in at an outdoor movie. Mickey Rooney was the attraction, in *A Yank at Eton,* and the dilemmas of an American in so outlandish a setting as England evoked enormous and completely unselfconscious mirth from a large and appreciative audience of Yanks.

We were awakened at four o'clock and took off at dawn. During the night a plane heading for Australia had come in. It was leaving about the same time we were, and the passengers of the two ships got mixed up while riding on trucks from the barracks to the field. After a lot of good-natured kidding, we were unscrambled, and nobody got on the wrong plane. We were in the air on this lap for about eight hours, which was time enough for us to polish off most of one of my chickens.

The island we were heading for was so tiny that when we circled over it, we found it hard to believe that a plane could land on it or that there was any life on it. It looked like a small sandspit. When we came down, we discovered that it was a little bigger than our estimate but not much. It was simply a piece of flat coral, so white that many of the soldiers stationed on it wore sunglasses, like skiers. From the air it had seemed deserted; on the ground we saw that it was a beautifully camouflaged military installation, bristling with guns and planes and men, some of whom had been living there for six months. There were no people on the island except soldiers —not even an Army nurse—but it had a few comforts. There was a club with an elegant dice table and a modest bar, which had a limit of four bottles of warm beer to a customer, no Coca-Cola, and grapefruit juice, for some reason or other, on the house. There were no grapefruit trees on the island. In fact, there was only one tree of any kind, a scraggly, stunted palm whose days appeared to be numbered.

We remained on the island for the afternoon, then had an excellent steak dinner before we left at dusk. Our pilot was figuring on hitting Hawaii, our last stop, just after daybreak the next morning. For a while, though, it looked doubtful whether we were going to leave that night at all. As we were getting ready to take off, two details of soldiers showed up at the landing field simultaneously. One group had seemingly been assigned to help us take off and the other to guard the plane overnight. The guards, the more confident of the two factions, had brought along cots, which they set up under the left wing. The ground crew stood around under the right wing, waiting to pull the chocks out from underneath the wheels. We passengers watched all this rather uncertainly. Finally the pilot and the rest of the plane crew drove up in a jeep, got into the plane, and started up the motors. The guard detail quietly folded up its cots and marched away.

We flew all night, sleeping most of the time, and reached Hawaii, as scheduled, in time for a late breakfast, with as many eggs as we wanted. We spent the day there, looking at Pearl Harbor, the barbed wire along Waikiki, the sailors quartered at the Royal Hawaiian, and the local belles. When we went back to the plane after supper, we found to our dismay that all the seats except one, which naturally went to the general, had been replaced by the mailbags. We had left our baggage on the plane. It was inextricably buried beneath the bags, and we never again caught sight of what then remained of my second chicken. Some new passengers joined us: a sergeant flying home to see a dying father, and a colonel in the Signal Corps. The colonel settled himself on some sacks of V-mail across the aisle from me. The particular bags on which I attempted to make myself at home were filled, I soon concluded, with metal pieces of enemy planes being sent home as souvenirs, or perhaps with jagged fragments of coral reefs. I sat on them throughout the night and the next morning, occasionally falling asleep and invariably, when I did, putting my feet in the colonel's face. At intervals he pushed at my legs and I woke up, apologized, and tried to assume a more agreeable position. It was bitterly cold, and we were all grateful when daylight arrived.

Shortly before noon, we flew above an island off the coast of California and circled gaily over it. A little while later, we saw the Golden Gate, which we had so often dreamed of sailing under. It looks good from any angle.

A Note About the Author

E. J. KAHN, JR., was selected to serve in the Army five months before Pearl Harbor. He left the United States in April, 1942, and spent nearly a year in the Southwest Pacific. He is now a Warrant Officer and is stationed in the Caribbean Area.

After his graduation from Harvard in 1937, Kahn worked on the staff of *The New Yorker* until his induction. He is the author of *The Army Life*, published in November, 1942.